Classic Camper Vans –
The Inside Story
A Guide to Classic British Campers 1956–1979

Classic Camper Vans – The Inside Story

A Guide to Classic British Campers 1956–1979

Martin Watts

The Crowood Press

First published in 2007 by

The Crowood Press Ltd

Ramsbury, Marlborough

Wiltshire SN8 2HR

www.crowood.com

British Library Cataloguing-in-Publication Data

A catalogue record for this book is available from the British Library.

ISBN 978 1 86126 947 8

Disclaimer

Some words, model names and designations are trademarked and are the property of the trademark owner. They have been used for identification purposes only and this is not an official publication.

Whilst every effort has been made to ensure the accuracy of all material, the author and publisher cannot accept liability for loss resulting from any error, mis-statement, inaccuracy or omission contained herein. The author welcomes any corrections or additional information.

Typeset and designed by D & N Publishing

Lambourn Woodlands, Hungerford, Berkshire.

Printed and bound in Singapore by Craft Print International.

contents

dedication

This book is dedicated to my wife Dilys for her undying support, and to my father Perry for his initial inspiration that guided me into the world of motorcaravanning.

acknowledgements

This book has been compiled with the help and assistance of many people from the world of motorcaravanning in the UK. In particular I would like to thank the family of the late John Hunt for allowing me to use many photographs from John's personal collection. In addition I would like to record my thanks to all the owners of period and classic campers who have assisted me with information and allowed me to photograph their beloved vehicles.

A special word of thanks is due to all past authors who have so skilfully recorded the models, events, price guides and definitive information so vital in both the research and preparation of this book. My thanks also to John de Mierre of the Motorhome Information Service (MIS) for kindly supplying some of the production records used in this book.

Most of the photographs and press pictures used in this book came from the archive of the author. The following people kindly supplied other photographs used: David Kesteven, Alan Kirtley, Tony Fernley, Chris Burlace, Steve Cooper, Rob Goodwin, Nick Stoton, John Hanson. I would like to record my thanks to Richard and Heather Holdsworth for allowing me to reproduce photographs of their conversions.

I should also thank any owner, not mentioned above, who may have gifted me photographs over the years to use as I see fit. Many owners have given or sent me valuable archive material in the form of books, sales brochures, photographs, price guides and newspaper cuttings. Although I have never recorded these people by name (there were quite simply far too many individuals), they will of course be well aware of whom they are upon reading this dedication. Their kindness has allowed me to put together a valuable archive of camper material from years gone by, so my sincere thanks to them all.

MARTIN WATTS, 2007

1

introduction

The epitome of the words 'classic camper': the iconic Volkswagen. Given that they were produced in such large numbers, it is little wonder that they are still so popular today. The after-sales service offered by VW was also excellent, with a dealer network set up around the world. Today, there is hardly a replacement part that can't be obtained for all the VW models, from body panels to mechanical items.

Motorcaravanning as a leisure activity has been in evidence in Britain since the end of the nineteenth century when the petrol engine was first developed. Several entrepreneurs and coachbuilding companies produced motorized caravans on the chassis available at the time, with varying degrees of success. Some of these early examples are highlighted below, giving a brief insight into motorcaravan development through the first half of the twentieth century. The prime objective of this book, however, is to take an in-depth look at the most popular motorcaravans in the UK from the mid-1950s through to the late 1970s, paying particular attention to the 'boom years' of sales in the UK during the 'swinging sixties'. Production figures from that period have never

been equalled by the industry to this day. Studies reveal that in comparable financial terms a motorcaravan built today is in fact better value than one produced forty years ago and thankfully the industry within the UK is once again growing year on year.

Interest in the motorhomes and campers produced since the 1950s has been increasing steadily in recent years. This is substantiated by the growing number of owners clubs now catering for the various marques and conversions, a growing number of dedicated Internet sites and the plethora of monthly publications now on sale. At the forefront of all this current 'classic camper' interest is the now famous offering from Germany, the VW van in its various forms. Whole industries have been born of

these models around the globe. There isn't a spare part or body panel that cannot be purchased in order to restore or rebuild a VW camper, and the amount of aftermarket accessories is also quite exhaustive. Many books have been written in recent years about the VW camper scene, and rightly so given the vehicle's popularity today. A being landing on Earth today from another planet could be forgiven for thinking that the VW camper was the only vehicle of its type produced during the 1950s, '60s and '70s, such is the publicity given over to it these days. Despite its popularity today, the mighty VW did not have things all its own way back in the classic years, as both the Bedford CA (in the 1950s) and the Rootes Commer (in the 1960s) sold in huge numbers.

RIGHT: One of the best-selling models in the UK during the 1950s was the Bedford Caravan by Martin Walter Ltd (Dormobile). Based on the Bedford CA, it would later become the Bedford Romany and introduce a generation to the joys of this versatile leisure activity. For many years after its introduction, people would quite wrongly refer to all motorcaravans as Dormobiles. However, this terminology has been replaced in recent years with the word 'camper'. Seen here is a Dormobile porthole model, circa 1958.

BELOW: An extremely popular base vehicle for conversion to camper in the early years was the BMC J2. Seen here is the Austin 152 variant with conversion by Auto-Conversions, later to become Car-Campers. The main difference between the Austin and Morris variants on the J2 were the slats on the front grille. The Austin seen here had horizontal slats, whereas those on the Morris version were vertical. The roof on this Austin Car-Camper is similar in style to the design employed by Westfalia on the VW models.

The marques already mentioned, together with such models as the Bedford CF, BMC J2, Ford Transit and Thames, Land Rover, Mercedes, Renault and Standard were all very popular base vehicles in years gone by. All of these famous marques will feature within this book, together with all the conversion companies such as Auto-Sleepers, Cotswold, Bluebird, Devon, Dormobile, Jennings and a whole host of others, some familiar and many that disappeared as quickly as they came.

Various owners clubs have been set up in the UK to cater for the owners of classic motorhomes and campers. It is largely thanks to such enthusiasts that a very large number of models have survived the test of time so that we can all enjoy them at events around the country throughout the year. I would like to thank these owners for allowing me to photograph their vehicles and for giving me their time to chat about their beloved 'vans during my research.

TYPES OF MOTORCARAVAN

There has been debate about the accepted terminology for the 'motorcaravan' since the end of the nineteenth century – which word best describes this particular type of vehicle? Terms of reference since that time have included: house car, camping car, motorized caravan, motorhome, motor caravan (also motorcaravan), camper and campervan. The two terms most widely used today are motorcaravan and camper; throughout this book I will refer to this particular type of vehicle as 'motorcaravan', the term widely adopted by the leading specialist publications on sale in the UK. Having clarified the terminology for this type of vehicle I now need to explain the different types of motorcaravan, which are divided into several categories. Firstly, there are the panel van conversions, with or without a rising roof. These are basic vans produced by the manufacturers and familiar to everyone as goods delivery vehicles. Motorcaravan converters will then set about transforming these vans into motorcaravans by adding side windows, interior furniture and other refinements one would expect to find in a leisure vehicle. Some of these vehicles will have a rising (or elevating) roof added to them by the converter; others will remain as fixed-roof examples (as was often the case with many early VW models). Since the early 1970s converters also began to remove the metal factory roof and fit a high-top roof made from GRP (glass-reinforced plastic, or fibreglass). This was/is done to afford the occupants full interior standing height. These models are referred to as high-top panel van conversions.

Next come the coach-built examples. This type of motorcaravan arrives at the converters simply as a chassis cab; the converters then coach-built a living area onto the chassis. This would often take the form of a timber frame, which was then covered in aluminium sheets and moulded GRP panels. An entrance door would then be incorporated in either the rear or side of the living area. The benefit of this type of model was that it afforded the occupants full standing height over the entire living area and, due to the extra space, converters would often incorporate a toilet/shower cubicle within the floor space.

Following on from the coach-built models are the often larger A-class examples. These models involved a similar construction process to the coach-built models, except that instead of the converters using a chassis cab they would begin the construction process using only the chassis, with no manufacturer's cab attached. The A-class style of motorcaravan has become very popular today, but within the classic years this principle of construction was in fact rarely used except for perhaps one-off models.

Another type or style of motorcaravan that only became popular during the latter classic period was the demountable (or dismountable) unit. In this instance, a coach-built living box was constructed that could be secured onto the back of a pick-up chassis or pick-up truck. When on site, securing legs would be fixed in place so that the unit became free-standing and the vehicle could be driven away.

EARLY PIONEERS OF THE MOTORIZED CARAVAN

When the nomadic spirit met the internal combustion engine a wanderlust dream was realized. With the advent of commercial vehicles the motorized caravan was born.

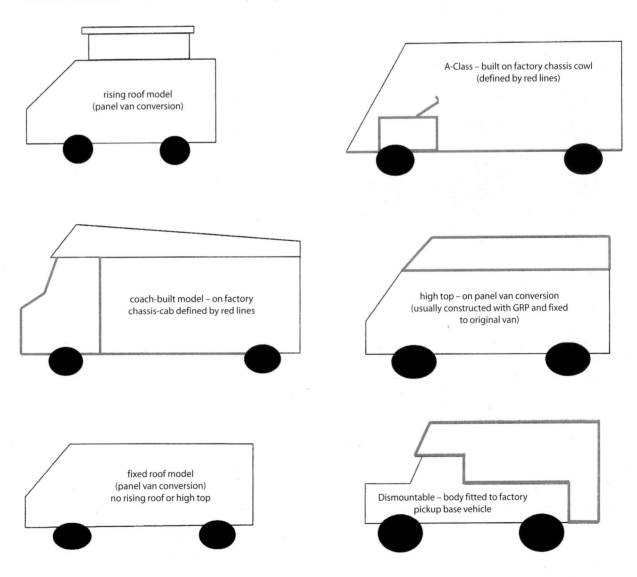

Camper type outlines.

One of the earliest references to motorcaravans to be recorded was that in *Autocar* magazine dating from August 1896, although there was no mention of the gentleman's name or picture of his proposed home on wheels with motorized power. It was stated that he was planning a four-roomed house with a collapsible upper storey to enable him to pass under bridges. The writer of the article obviously had great vision when he wrote, 'In the near future, we are likely to have large and decent house-cars, readily movable at will, and without calling in the aid of draught-horses or traction engines'. The author really must have had a crystal ball because the motor vehicle was very much in its infancy at this stage. Just thirteen years later, at the 1909 Motor Show (based at Olympia), the Austin Motor Company displayed a 40hp van with semi-forward control. Austin had built no ordinary van, as this one was constructed for Mr Arthur Du Cros, of Dunlop fame. The vehicle was not a tremendous success with the public and few, if any, were in fact sold. It does, however, leave the Austin Company with one claim to fame at least within the UK leisure industry; they were the first motor company to build its own motorcaravan from the ground up. The first UK company believed to have produced 'popular' motorized living vans was Duntons of Reading. The company had been Romany wagon builders and had

successfully married caravan bodies to the Model T Ford.

The company in this country to produce the first purpose-built motorcaravans was Eccles. W.A.J. Riley built his first motorcaravan just prior to World War I, but the Eccles story really began once the war was over. The haulage firm of Eccles Motor Transport Ltd was in a rather run-down state when Mr Riley took it over from Mr Eccles in 1919. A good reputation for quality was quickly established both for caravan and motorcaravan components and the company began to flourish. During 1926 the company changed its name to Eccles Motorcaravans Ltd and company advertisements were soon to be seen in the popular motoring journals of the time.

A basic range of two conversions was available bearing the Eccles logo, one on the Model T Ford and the other on the Chevrolet LT chassis. Considered to be somewhat box-like in appearance, the Ford-based model featured bay windows on each side and a rather distinctive stove chimney crowning the vehicle roofline. Rather more pleasing to the eye was the model derived from the Chevrolet truck chassis, which was altogether more sculptured and streamlined. The Chevrolet incorporated the same Mollicroft roof as used on the Eccles caravans, together with additional features such as leaded windows. During the 1930s the trailer caravan was proving to be far more popular than

its motorized counterpart, and Eccles decided to concentrate its efforts on the caravans. The company continued in production until 1960, when it was taken over by the larger Sprite concern.

Several companies had entered into the production of motorcaravans during the 1920s and 1930s, including the Car-Cruiser Company owned by Mr C. Flemming-Williams. This operation was founded in 1925 and soon established a reputation for building extremely light motorcaravans and caravans. Car-Cruiser's, like Eccles, eventually concentrated solely on trailer caravan production until ceasing trading in 1965.

Undoubtedly the 1930s had been a turning point in the history of production motorcaravans, and indeed caravans, in Britain. It was, however, to be trailer caravans that captured the imagination of the public, with some innovative and affordable models being produced. By 1932 *Autocar* magazine was featuring a regular column about caravans and in 1933 the world's first specialist caravan magazine was born. In contrast, it would be many years later, 1966 to be precise, before the first motorcaravan magazine was to go on sale to the general public.

In conclusion, although several coach-building companies were producing motorcaravans in limited numbers throughout the 1920s, '30s and '40s, it would not be until the mid-1950s that motorized caravans found favour with the public in the UK.

Eccles is widely recognized as being one of the first UK companies to produce motorcaravans in any great number. Eccles Motorcaravans produced many quality models during the 1920s and into the early '30s. The company later concentrated far more on trailer caravan production as touring caravans became more popular. Seen here is an early Eccles motorcaravan.

NO SMOKING

THE 10,000TH BEDFORD CONVERSION OFF THE LINE SINCE JANUARY 1959

2 *post-World War II production to 1960*

No UK company was better at producing campers in huge numbers during the 1950s than Martin Walter Ltd. However, don't be misled by the proclamation sign atop the Bedford camper, as the company produced not only Bedford campers but also general utility vehicles, mobile shops and personnel carriers, all based on the Bedford CA van. Sadly, no production figures survive from the period defining exactly how many of those 10,000 conversions were in fact campers.

The well-established coachbuilders Martin Walter Ltd of Folkestone was the first UK company (post-war) to offer a utility vehicle. This was based on the Bedford CA released in 1952 and featured the company's Dormatic seating arrangement. It was basically a Bedford van for carrying several passengers that could quickly and easily be adapted as a sleeping vehicle. It didn't feature any interior fitments and certainly had no cooking or washing facilities on board. The Folkestone company had been in operation since 1773 as saddle and harness makers, in time progressing to being coachbuilders. Martin Walter, the founder's grandson, together

with his brother-in-law Spencer Apps, transformed the business into a limited company. In 1911 Martin Walter Ltd was born; soon after, it acquired the local coachbuilding company Hills & Co. Later, the company began to make specialist bodies for the likes of Rolls-Royce, Daimler, Mercedes and Vauxhall. By 1935 the company was producing its Utilicon vehicle, suitably designed to carry both passengers and goods. It is believed that Spencer Apps had spotted people sleeping in their cars while they were waiting to catch the nearby cross-channel ferry. He came up with the idea of fitting out a vehicle with dual-purpose seats that could also form a bed. Company Director Lyne-Smith is credited with coming up with the Latin-derived name, Dormobile. By the mid-1950s the first fully fitted Dormobile, together with its rising roof, would quickly become the biggest selling motorcaravan in the UK.

It is during this period (1955–57) that historians beg to differ on the question

of which company did what first. There is little doubt that Martin Walter Ltd was the first UK company to offer a dual-purpose vehicle. It is, though, most likely that German refugee Peter Pitt (based in north London) was the first to offer a completely fitted motorcaravan for sale; that is to say, interior fitments including cupboards, beds/seating, cooker and sink. Peter required a utility vehicle for his photographic business and his range of Moto-Caravan models were ingenious and exciting in their interior design. The open-plan layout that he pioneered became very popular, not least because of his use of the interior proportions of the van. Peter's early motorcaravans were based on the VW and had no rising roof. Sadly, Peter Pitt never did receive the recognition he so rightly deserved for his clever designs and it is the part that he played in altering the law of the day for which he will best be remembered.

Peter believed that a motorcaravan should be taxed as a car and subjected

This advertisement for Pitt campers dates from 1959; at this time he was offering conversions on the BMC J2, Ford Thames and the VW. The Peter Pitt designs were rather ingenious, allowing the internal fitments to be moved around to suit the occupants. This open-plan layout would continue to be used throughout the 1960s, even under the Canterbury-Pitt banner.

to similar speed limits, despite its light commercial chassis. He further believed that a motorcaravan should share the tax advantages of a trailer caravan and be exempted from purchase tax.

In order that a motorcaravan owner could enjoy the best of both worlds a change in the law would be required. Peter was quite prepared to test this out in the Courts; it would also double up as good publicity for his Moto-Caravan models! At this time (1957–58), commercial vehicles not allowed in the Royal Parks at Windsor, so this was the ideal location in which to test his theory. He drove his VW motorcaravan through the park and, just as he had anticipated, the Police duly prosecuted him. It remains unclear if the case actually went to Court, but certainly from that moment on motorcaravans could travel at the same speed as a car on the open road, with the benefit of being exempt from purchase tax.

Having already mentioned that there are conflicting thoughts about who did what and when during this period, there is well-documented proof that Maurice Calthorpe was the first to fit a rising roof to a motorcaravan (in the UK). This though was not the type to become

such a familiar sight in the ensuing years, the version first designed and built by Maurice was constructed using both aluminium and wood. It was pushed up from inside the vehicle to form a narrow arched area to allow full standing height. Within months of Maurice introducing his rising roof, Martin Walter Ltd had fitted its first side-hinged rising roof to a Bedford CA (this initial design was much smaller than the later versions). The subject of the rising (or elevating) roof is quite fascinating in the context of these early motorcaravans and will be looked at in greater detail later.

Pre-war Britain had given the introduction of motorized caravans only a lukewarm reception; post-war however, things were altogether a different story and this new arm of the leisure industry was to prove far more successful for those pioneering manufacturers. Two of the leading entrepreneurs, Peter Pitt and Maurice Calthorpe, had great design ideas but limited finances. It was therefore hardly surprising that Martin Walter Ltd (Dormobile) was quick to establish itself as the leading builder of motorcaravans in the UK. It already had huge factory premises in Folkestone, a workforce of experienced staff and

in-house designers, not to mention many years of coachbuilding expertise. The company's Bedford Caravan (later to become the Bedford Romany) became a firm favourite with the motorcaravan-buying public and quickly established itself as the best-selling motorcaravan in the UK in a very short space of time.

THE FIRST POST-WAR COACH-BUILT MOTORCARAVAN

Having already mentioned that Maurice Calthorpe is credited with producing the first rising roof in the UK, it is also important to record that in 1957 he was responsible for producing the first coach-built model. He based this on the Bedford CA chassis cab. The model retained only the front section of the Bedford cab (grille, bonnet, wings and windscreen), with the result that the whole vehicle, when complete, was rather box-like in appearance.

Despite being a coach-built model, this Calthorpe Home Cruiser only had an interior standing height of 4ft 8in (1,372mm), increasing to 6ft 1in (1,854mm) with the roof raised. One wonders why Calthorpe went through the time and expense of producing a

RIGHT: Kenex of Dover was an already established coachbuilder when it entered the motorcaravan market at the end of the 1950s. The company offered its Carefree range upon a variety of different chassis including the Bedford CAS/CAL, Ford Thames and Standard Atlas. Its models featured a very distinctive rising roof.

BELOW: Wessex Motors of Wiltshire introduced the Car-O-Van based on the BMC J2 in 1958. Internally, the camper featured mahogany fittings and had a rather stylish rising roof with solid sides and fitted windows. Sadly, this model appears to have disappeared from the scene almost as quickly as it arrived. This picture is clearly a staged promotion shot as there is no registration plate visible on the rear of the vehicle.

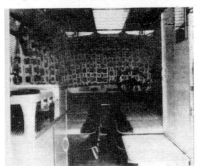

Make yourself at
HOME ANYWHERE

with the
KENEX *Carefree*

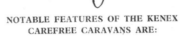

NOTABLE FEATURES OF THE KENEX CAREFREE CARAVANS ARE:

Special luxury seating converting easily into beds.
Four berths.
Easy-lifting roof giving six feet headroom.
Two-burner gas cooker and grill.
Sink unit and seven-gallon water tank.
Gas and electric light.

Prices

BEDFORD CAS (Standard)	...	£780.0.0
(De Luxe)	...	£843.0.0
BEDFORD CAL (Standard)	...	£805.0.0
(De Luxe)	...	£868.0.0
STANDARD ATLAS CAREFREE		£810.0.0

SEE YOUR LOCAL BEDFORD & STANDARD DEALER FOR FULL DETAILS.

RIGHT: *Maurice Calthorpe built the first post-World War II production coach-built examples in 1957. Based on the Bedford CA, they still made use of the Calthorpe rising roof, despite being a coach-build. It is believed that only a handful were sold, in spite of bringing in female personality Dora Bryan to film a Pathe News promotional film. This is how the original Home Cruiser looked back in 1957.*

BELOW: *For many years it was believed that none of the original Calthorpe models had survived, until 2006 when an eagle-eyed reader spotted an advertisement in a specialist classic commercial magazine. Motorcaravan historian John Hanson recognized it and made contact with me. This set in motion a chain of events that led to the rescue of such an important classic camper and it is now in the hands of a Bedford enthusiast who plans to restore it. It is seen here up on ramps soon after being rescued from a lock-up garage in Kew, where it had stood since the early 1970s.*

coach-built example and then fitting it with a rising roof. Maurice himself must have come to the same conclusion, as only a handful of the Home Cruiser coach-built models were ever produced. Calthorpe swiftly switched his conversion to Bedford panel vans, retaining his patented rising roof. The coach-built Home Cruiser carried a price tag of £945 in August 1957.

Until the spring of 2006 it was believed that none of the handful of Home Cruisers produced during 1957 had survived, until a very fuzzy picture of one appeared in an advertisement in a monthly magazine. I only came upon this rare find some months later and telephoned the number given in order to find out who had purchased it. Much to my amazement, the vehicle was still in the lock-up where it had been for around thirty years. A Bedford enthusiast and myself tried in vain to convince the owner of the historical importance of this motorcaravan. Negotiations eventually broke down and the owner stated that the vehicle would go for scrap. Some months later, this 1957 example reappeared in the hands of a Bedford parts specialist, who had been offered the vehicle by a London-based scrapyard owner. Thank goodness the owner of the scrapyard had realized the importance of this vehicle and spared it from the crusher. The only known surviving Home Cruiser coach-build has now been purchased by a museum and is being restored to its former glory.

A full road test of this particular model appeared in *Motor* magazine, dated 28 August 1957. *Pathe News* also filmed a picnic trip with this Home Cruiser in 1957; the film includes appearances by both Maurice Calthorpe and radio and television personality Dora Bryan. The clip also shows a female model using the bath that was fitted beneath the bench-style cab seats!

MORE COACH-BUILT MODELS FROM THE 1950s

Maurice Calthorpe was only just first in line with a coach-built model in 1957; within months of his Home Cruiser appearing, the cunningly named Paralanian was introduced. Central Garage Ltd of Bradford built this model. The company was based in Parry Lane, hence the clever use of words to determine a name for the new motorcaravan.

The Paralanian was the brainchild of Works Director Clifford Hobson, an ex-naval captain. He assembled a team to design and construct a motorcaravan. Work commenced early in 1957 and the model was released before the end of the year. This model was constructed upon an ash frame with a wonderful interior of polished walnut. The company brochure used such sales quotes as, 'If you own a Rolls-Royce you'll be proud of this too'. An advertisement in *Motor* around this time proclaimed, 'Your home from home'.

A local Bradford photographer, Eric Alderton, was loaned a prototype model for several weeks in order to make a film featuring the Paralanian for promotional purposes. The completed film, lasting around twenty minutes, was entitled *Overland to Athens* and was shown at the Motor Show. This early Paralanian was of conventional box-like appearance and featured Venetian blinds to the large side windows, a full oven, a fitted Axminster carpet and a chemical toilet housed in a small toilet compartment. The price back then reflected the quality of this model – £1,050 for the standard Paralanian and £1,250 for the Deluxe, very serious money indeed for 1957! The Paralanian was built on the Austin 152 chassis.

Released a year after the Calthorpe Home Cruiser and Paralanian was the Bluebird Highwayman. In external appearance the Highwayman was very similar to the Paralanian, but there the similarity ends. The build quality of this model was far inferior to the Paralanian, the principal aim being the new hire market. The Highwayman became an overnight success, although this was

ABOVE: Marketed as the most luxurious production motorcaravan in the UK from 1957, the Paralanian was a lesson in high-quality craftsmanship. The MK I and MK II models were of a square external appearance and had a single rear entrance door. This is the very early version, a MK I.

BELOW: Early Bluebird Highwayman, very similar in external appearance to the first Paralanian models, but not of a similar quality internally.

KEY

1   wardrobe, which converts into a toilet area
2   gas light
3   sink/drainer with lift-up worktop
4   eye-level storage lockers
5   cooker with full oven and storage under
6   storage area for table (behind back seat)
7   dinette converted to a small double bed (gas-bottle storage underneath one seat)
8   single stretcher bunk and large storage area over cab
9   seat backs were removable to form centre panels for bed
10   a pull-out double bed with storage underneath (long settee during the day)
11   drawers with storage cupboards above

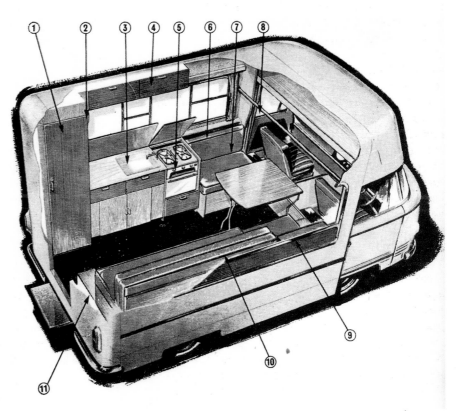

largely due to the foresight of one man, Peter Duff. Peter was the Managing Director of Crofton Garages in London; they were BMC agents looking to expand their business. At around this time, Maurice Calthorpe was seeking a London distributor for his Home Cruiser range and Peter agreed a deal to sell them. As a result of this link-up, Crofton would staff Calthorpe's 1959 Motor Show stand. At around the same time,

Peter Duff first saw the Highwayman and agreed a deal with Bluebird, becoming the Metropolitan distributor for the model. The success of the Highwayman went from strength to strength, firstly based on the BMC J2 chassis and later the Commer. It went on to become the biggest-selling coach-built motorcaravan in the UK throughout the 1960s and '70s. The Highwayman carried a price tag of around £800 during the late 1950s.

EARLY PANEL VAN CONVERSIONS

Mentioned above are some of the early motorcaravan pioneers such as Peter Pitt, Maurice Calthorpe and Martin Walter Ltd (Dormobile). These were certainly the first to offer panel van conversions during the 1950s in the UK, but also worth mentioning here is J.P. White (Jack White of Sidmouth, Lisburne Garages), which began converting the VW around 1957.

From 1958, more converters entered the market: Taylor Motor Body Conversions of Norfolk with its Bedmobile based on the Bedford CA; Auto

LEFT: Superlite Caravans produced this panel van conversion during the late 1950s on a Ford Thames. The unusual high roof was not of the rising type, but fixed in position. Little is known of the conversion itself, as Superlite did not feature in the buyer's guides of the period.
BELOW: Locomotors produced this quite unique coach-built example on the BMC J2. Given the name Space Traveller, it was rather futuristic for 1960 with its wrap-around windows and use of GRP for external bodywork. Rear corners were also nicely contoured with rolled aluminium sheeting instead of a square finish.

RIGHT: Internally, the Space Traveller reverted from futuristic to the status quo, the designers opting for a tried and trusted layout rather than trying to match the external styling. The female model is clearly demonstrating the fact that full standing height was a benefit of the Space Traveller.

BELOW: J. P. White Ltd of Sidmouth is well known to early VW enthusiasts for its Devon conversions. The company also produced the popular Sleep-A-Kar conversions of the late 1950s on the BMC J2 range.

Conversions of Birmingham released the Car-Camper on the BMC J2; Moortown Motors of Leeds produced the Moortown VW; Service Garages in Essex released the Service VW; European Cars of London brought out the Slumberwagon VW; and Wessex Motors in Wiltshire introduced the Wessex Carovaner, based on the BMC J2. Yet despite so many more motorcaravans being introduced, it was to remain the Martin Walter factory at Folkestone that built the lion's share of motorcaravans for the UK market, by some considerable margin. Walker's Bedford Caravan, based on the popular CA van, won the hearts of the public. Several factors contributed to this, notably the 'value for money' package, excellent advertising, a tried-and-trusted base vehicle and little or no delay in delivery time due to the sheer numbers being built. That initial Bedford Caravan introduced a generation to the joys of outdoor living and touring and within a short time it became known quite simply as the Dormobile. This happened to such an extent that for many years afterwards (probably into the 1990s), people wrongly referred to all motorcaravans as Dormobiles.

Home comforts
on four wheels in the luxurious
COMMER CARAVAN
PETROL OR DIESEL

3 *base vehicle specifications*

The Commer Caravan was Rootes' own camper conversion based on its 1500 minibus chassis with side and rear doors. A very popular panel van camper from 1960 to 1965, Rootes (by then Chrysler) ceased production in order to supply Commer chassis for the extremely successful Highwayman.

The base vehicles used for motorcaravan construction were rather limited in the UK when this leisure activity first grabbed the public's imagination. During the mid-1950s converters had only a handful of chassis from which to choose. These included the Bedford CA, BMC J2, Ford Thames and the VW Microbus and Kombi. The little Standard Atlas joined this list from 1958. These base vehicles really did have something of a monopoly until the introduction of the Rootes Commer 1500 in 1960. Rootes also became the first manufacturer (post-World War II) to carry out its own conversion; released as the Commer Caravan, this conversion became affectionately known as the Commer-Commer. The start of the 1960s also saw another new entrant into the base vehicle stakes, the BMC J4. But despite its popularity as a delivery goods van, it never really found favour with motorcaravan converters.

The base vehicle options would remain pretty much unchanged until the introduction of a motoring legend in 1965, the Ford Transit.

Since its introduction in 1960, the Rootes Commer 1500 (Chrysler Commer from 1964) had become the number one choice as a base vehicle for motorcaravan construction, but the new offering from Ford was about to change all that. The new Transit could not have been more different from its predecessor, the Thames. Here at last was a light commercial van which actually had car-like handling, very comfortable seating and later came in a bewildering array of engine and body options.

From this point, until 1969 there was once again a period of status quo with the Bedford CA, BMC J2 (ceased production in 1967), Commer and the VW (the panel van model now being the converters' choice over the earlier Microbus and Kombi) providing the

majority of the base vehicles. A couple of months after man first landed on the moon came a new model to replace the ageing Bedford CA. The Bedford CF had arrived and made an immediate impact upon the motorcaravan market. Martin Walter Ltd (Dormobile) had remained so loyal to the Bedford brand that Dormobile models on the new CF were in fact unveiled before the official launch of the whole CF range! Converters welcomed the new CF with open arms; in a league table of sales for this period it was now the Bedford CF, Commer, Ford Transit and VW way out in front.

It should be emphasized how many BMC base vehicles were being utilized. Out of all the manufacturers, BMC certainly had the most models available. The Austin 152/Morris J2 (commonly referred to as the J2 range) finished production in 1967; the model was replaced with the BMC 250JU. Due to company amalgamations (and a little badge engineering), the Standard Atlas ceased production in 1962 but reappeared immediately as the Leyland 20 (which in turn was deleted in 1968). The BMC J4 model was introduced in 1960, continued in production until 1974, then became (with some modifications) the Leyland Sherpa. When mentioning the BMC (later BLMC) model list, one should not forget that the original Mini was actually a motorcaravan base vehicle. Less than a handful of such models were ever marketed utilizing this vehicle though, with the Wildgoose probably being the most successful. On the subject of small BMC/BLMC base vehicles one simply can't forget the Torcars Company in Devon. It began in 1968, producing a conversion on the very small BMC half-ton van (named the Sun-Tor); when the half-ton van ceased production in the early 1970s, the company began converting the new Marina van (listed as the Marina Sun-Tor).

The other popular base vehicles utilized during the 1970s were the Bedford HA, the Ford Escort van, the Fiat 850/900 van, Land Rover, Mercedes 206 and the MK I Toyota Hiace.

BACKGROUND HISTORY OF THE MOST POPULAR BASE VEHICLES

Undoubtedly the most popular base vehicles used for motorcaravan conversion are small in number. Many of the best-selling motorcaravans of the classic period were based on just five vehicles, the Bedford CA and CF, BMC J2 (Austin and Morris), Commer PA/PB and the Ford Transit. Deliberately omitted are the evergreen VW bases, even though they were a firm favourite with buyers during this period. The reason for this is that so much written material is already in the public domain, in the form of various books and manuals (the excellent publication from The Crowood Press, *VW Camper – The Inside Story*, by David Eccles, being a classic example). This section of the book will therefore provide a more detailed insight into the five leading base vehicles and specification changes during their production.

Bedford CA

Vauxhall Motors of Luton introduced this light commercial van in April 1952

in 10/12cwt forms (a 15cwt model was released in 1958) and it quickly established itself as a very popular delivery vehicle. It enjoyed a seventeen-year production run, before being replaced by the Bedford CF in 1969.

The Bedford CA was a model that was constantly updated throughout production, the most noticeable external modification being the windscreen. When released, the CA was fitted with a two-piece split screen; this was replaced by a one-piece screen in 1959, together with a redesigned front grille. The windscreen was widened again by June of the same year; it would remain at this size until 1964, when it was increased again in height and width.

As far as the power plant was concerned, the CA began with a 1508cc petrol unit (1952–63), which in turn was replaced by a larger 1595cc engine from 1963. Two diesel engines were offered

as options during CA production; these were firstly the Perkins 4.99 (from June 1961) and later (1965 onwards) the Perkins 4.108. The wheels fitted to the CA were altered, beginning with 16in upon its release, changing to 15in in 1957. By 1960 the sizes had been changed once again when the smaller 13in was introduced.

From the outset in 1952 the CA was constantly updated and modified, including engine size alterations, wheels, body and mechanical changes. The biggest of these changes came in 1964 when the MK II version was announced (although not introduced until May of 1965). All CA variants featured three- and four-speed column-mounted gear change. The CA range was discontinued in 1969 when the all-new CF range was introduced.

The CA, despite being a very popular delivery vehicle, only gained such an

The BMC J2 in both Austin 152 and Morris J2 variants was used extensively during the 1950s by various converters. Martin Walter Ltd also applied its Dormobile design to the BMC chassis, fitting its famous side-hinged roof. In this early 1960s advertisement the company is clearly making the point that this Austin 152 Dormobile would be the ideal mode of transport for that holiday on the continent.

Popular Base Vehicles/Chassis Specifications

Bedford CA 1952–69

ENGINE: 1508cc, 1595cc petrol engines (four-cylinder diesel option available)
TRANSMISSION: three- and four-speed column-mounted change

Bedford CF 1969–87
ENGINE (PETROL): 1599cc, 1975cc, 1759cc, 2279cc petrol engines
ENGINE (DIESEL): 1760cc (Perkins), 2064cc (GM) and 2260cc from 1980
TRANSMISSION: four-speed floor-mounted change as standard; overdrive option on the CF250 petrol model. Five-speed ZF gearbox was optional on the CF280, CF350 and CF350L models. A GM three-speed automatic box was optional on all but the CF350 and CF350L models

Bedford HA 1964–82
ENGINE: 1256cc petrol engine
TRANSMISSION: four-speed floor-mounted change

BMC (including later BLMC and Leyland models) Austin 152 (and Morris J2) 1956–67
ENGINES: 1489cc and 1622cc petrol (diesel option available)
TRANSMISSION: four-speed column-mounted change

Austin J4 (also badged as Morris and BMC) 1960–74
ENGINES: 1622cc petrol (1489cc diesel option available)
TRANSMISSION: four-speed floor-mounted change

BMC 250JU (renamed Austin-Morris in 1970) 1967–74
ENGINES: as for J2 and J4 models, but engine was relocated at an angle beneath front seats
TRANSMISSION: four-speed

BMC Mini (only used for conversion during the 1960s)
ENGINE: 848cc petrol engine
TRANSMISSION: four-speed floor-mounted change

BMC half-ton van (badged as Austin A55 and Morris A60) 1958–71
ENGINE: 1622cc petrol engine
TRANSMISSION: four-speed column-mounted change

BL Marina
ENGINE: 1275cc petrol engine
TRANSMISSION: four-speed floor-mounted change

Leyland Sherpa 1975–81
(then renamed the Freight Rover Sherpa)
ENGINE: 1622cc and 1798cc petrol (1798cc diesel option available)
TRANSMISSION: four-speed floor-mounted change (overdrive became an option on the 1798cc petrol models)

Standard Atlas (later renamed Leyland 20)
ENGINE: 948cc Standard petrol engine initially, later the 1630cc petrol unit and optional 2260cc diesel engine

Land Rover 1948–present
ENGINE: 2286cc petrol engine
TRANSMISSION: eight gears (4 × 4)

Commer PA/PB 1500 & 2500 1960–82
ENGINE: 1494cc, 1592cc, 1725cc petrol engines; Perkins diesel engine was an option
TRANSMISSION: four-speed floor-mounted change; overdrive an option on the 1725cc engine

Fiat 850T & 900T 1956–80
ENGINE: 903cc petrol unit
TRANSMISSION: four-speed floor-mounted change

Ford Escort (only the MK I & MK II models used for conversion) 1968–80
ENGINE: 1298cc petrol engine
TRANSMISSION: four-speed floor-mounted change

Ford Thames 12 & 15cwt range 1957–65
ENGINE: 1703cc petrol engine; Perkins diesel unit was an option
TRANSMISSION: three- and four-speed column-mounted change

Ford Transit 1965–present
ENGINE: petrol options were 1.6ltr, 1.7ltr, 2.0ltr, 2.5ltr and 3.0ltr; diesel options were Perkins 4/99 and 4/108, also the York 2.4ltr (these were the engine options offered during the classic years, as covered in this publication)
TRANSMISSION: four-speed floor-mounted change; optional overdrive on many engines

Mercedes (Hanomag-Henschel) L206D produced until 1977
ENGINE: 2.2ltr (2197cc) diesel
TRANSMISSION: four-speed floor-mounted change

Renault Estafette 1959–80
ENGINE: 845cc, 1108cc and 1289cc petrol engines
TRANSMISSION: four-speed floor-mounted change

Toyota Hiace
ENGINE: 1587cc petrol engine
TRANSMISSION: four-speed column-mounted change

Volkswagen (Kombi, Microbus and van) 1949–67 (splitscreen models) and 1967–79 (bay window models)
ENGINE: 1192cc, 1584cc, 1.7ltr, 1.8ltr and 2.0ltr petrol engines
TRANSMISSION: four-speed floor-mounted change

The base vehicles featured in the specifications listing represent the most popular used during the classic years of motorcaravan production. Not included are those that were used for one-off specials/custom builds and those used for very limited build runs.

When it came to base vehicles in the 1950s and '60s, the Bedford CA was certainly a top five contender. Martin Walter Ltd used the CA in huge numbers throughout its production from 1952 to 1969. Seen here is the base chassis of the Bedford CAL (long wheelbase) dating from 1962.

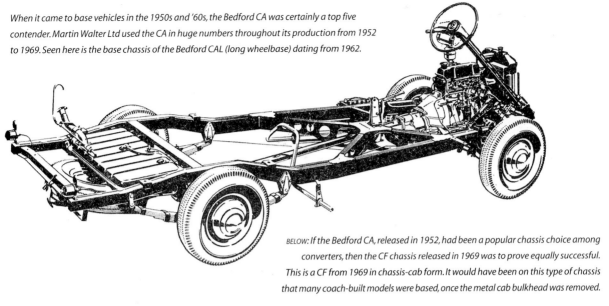

BELOW: If the Bedford CA, released in 1952, had been a popular chassis choice among converters, then the CF chassis released in 1969 was to prove equally successful. This is a CF from 1969 in chassis-cab form. It would have been on this type of chassis that many coach-built models were based, once the metal cab bulkhead was removed.

excellent reputation within motorcaravanning through the Dormobile conversions. Despite conversions by other companies such as the Hadrian, Calthorpe, Pegasus and Bedmobile, the CA will be forever associated with the great Folkestone company of Martin Walter Ltd (Dormobile).

Bedford CF

As previously mentioned, the CF model was a direct replacement for the CA. Initially, the CF range used the 1599cc and 1975cc petrol engines, with the Perkins 1760cc being the diesel option. By 1972, the petrol engine sizes had been increased to 1759cc and 2279cc. The engine position within the CF remained similar to the old CA model, being mounted half in the cab and half under the front bonnet. The option of sliding cab doors (as seen on the earlier CA) was again available on the CF range, though this feature on the CF in particular was more popular on goods delivery vans than those converted into motorcaravans.

Most motorcaravans were built on either the CF220 or CF250 bases. These numbers represented the gross vehicle weight (GVW), for example the 220 meant 2.20 ton. The designation badge was carried on the front wheel arch. The majority of motorcaravans were based on the single rear wheel CF bases, although some of the later, much larger coach-built examples used the twin rear wheelbase.

The CF range would continue to undergo minor alterations and modifications until 1980, when the CF was given a facelift. A plastic front grille was the most noticeable external change; the range was also modified and consisted of the CF230, 250, 280 and 350. This revamped model is often incorrectly referred to as the CF2, but the official CF2 was not introduced until 1984. The CF production run ended in 1987, having enjoyed an eighteen-year span.

The basic interior of a Bedford CF van. This was the view confronting the workforce at the various converters as they began their process of conversion from van to camper. The metal bulkhead behind the cab would have been omitted from the vans ordered by the conversion companies, in order to allow access from cab to living quarters and vice versa.

Just about every notable converter used the CF as a base during its production run, from Dormobile in 1969 through to the GRP-bodied examples from Auto-Sleepers in the 1980s.

BMC J2 (Austin and Morris Variants)

The J-series formed the basis of BMC's light commercial range, having its origins in the Morris Company. The Austin-Morris merger during the early 1950s would see such models as the LD, J2 and later 250JU designated as either Austin or Morris.

In 1956 the J2 15cwt model would be BMC's first unitary construction van. The company was famous for its 'badge engineering' and the J2 was to prove no exception, with both Austin and Morris examples being made available. The only real difference between the two was the lower front panel. Morris versions were given an inverted heart-shaped grille; Austin variants had a rectangular grille. Originally the range was fitted with the 1489cc B-series petrol engine, receiving the 1622cc engine in 1961. The range came with a four-speed gearbox as standard and a column-mounted gear change.

As with the majority of light commercials, the J2 was released in various forms, from pick-up, minibus to van. It was the minibus option that proved popular immediately with motorcaravan converters, as it came with side windows and a very convenient side-opening door, in addition to the one-piece rear door.

Memorable conversions on the J2 included such models as Auto-Sleeper, Car-Camper, Cotswold, Highwayman and Paralanian. The J2 was also very popular as a base for DIY conversions during the late 1950s and early 1960s.

Commer 1500/2500 PA/PB

The Commer 1500 forward-control light van was released in January 1960 and was originally powered by the 1494cc petrol engine. This was quickly found to be rather underpowered and was replaced by the 1592cc unit in 1961. The 1500 designation indicated the payload (three-quarter ton) and in 1962 it was joined in the model line-up by the 2500 (1 ton model payload). By 1964 the Rootes Company had linked up with the American Chrysler Corporation, so it then switched from being the Rootes Commer to the Chrysler Commer.

In 1965 the Commer was given a minor facelift – the successful 1725cc petrol engine was fitted as standard, the front grille was altered and it was given the PA designation. More changes would follow in 1967, when the handbrake was relocated from the rear wheels to the front wheels; from this point the PA became the PB.

Automatic transmission became available from 1965, the Commer having a four-speed floor-mounted gear change throughout production (an overdrive became available as an option during the 1970s). The option of a diesel engine was available; initially this was a Perkins 4.99 from 1960 and in 1965 the Perkins 4.108 was offered.

The Commer, having fallen under Chrysler control, would have two other

The Commer 1500/2500 enjoyed a twenty-two-year production run with only minimal changes to the basic body shape. It was available in various guises from basic panel van to pick-up, and minibus to chassis cab. In this picture it is possible to see the complete assembly view of upper body and lower engine and running gear.

owners before it ceased production in 1982. Firstly, the Peugeot Citroën PSA Group became custodians of the Commer brand, but in the final years Renault UK took over the Commer-Dodge mantle. The company now holds all production records for the Commer-Dodge vans.

In basic body shape, the Commer changed very little during its twenty-two-year production run. The most noticeable change took place in 1976 when the Commer was renamed the Dodge Spacevan. At this time, the front panel was altered, with chrome and aluminium trim giving way to plastic.

As with the Bedford CF and Ford Transit, just about every conversion company of note produced motorcaravan models on the Commer base (nearly fifty at last count!). Despite the popularity of the VW today, the Commer was the leading base motorcaravan throughout the 1960s. The Commer Highwayman by CI/M of Poole was the best-selling coach-built example in the 1960s and the early 1970s. The popularity of the Commer-Dodge Spacevan began to wane during the late 1970s, with the van remaining in production mainly due to large orders from the GPO (Post Office Telecommunications) for its bright yellow vans.

Ford Transit

The Transit name has become synonymous with light commercial vehicles since its launch back in 1965. The Transit was a direct replacement for the Thames, which had only been in production for a few years. The new Transit (also named the Thames upon its release) really did take the motorcaravan industry by storm, not to mention the warm reception it received from tradespeople. At the time of its introduction, no fewer than forty-four different versions, built on six models, were available. These ranged in payload capacity from 12cwt to 35cwt. The list of various bases available was equally as impressive; they included van, custom van, kombi, bus, custom bus, chassis cab, and custom chassis cab and chassis windshield. So varied were the Transit options that Ford claimed to offer one thousand bodywork options, adding that they could build over six million Transits without ever making two exactly the same.

The engines fitted to the Transit have been as varied as the bodywork options over the years, ranging from 1.7ltr to 3.0ltr petrol together with a variety of diesel options. To say that the Transit went through several modifications over the years would be a huge understatement, therefore only the more major changes will be highlighted here. Transmission on the Transit was four-speed floor-mounted gear change on all models; from 1967 a BorgWarner automatic gearbox became optionally available. In 1968 the interior cab layout was modified after Ford had conducted some extensive safety checks. The fascia was redesigned, heater controls repositioned, additional padding was fitted and rocker-type switches fitted. By June of 1968 Ford was offering the high-compression V4 2ltr engine (petrol), which would become the most common unit fitted in motorcaravan conversions. A bigger petrol engine became an option in 1974 with the 3.0ltr V6; front disc brakes were also added to the options' listing that year. The original MK I Transit would be a story of constant modification until 1978 when Ford announced the MK II model. The new Transit featured a completely new cab interior and restyling to the front cab panels, including the ubiquitous 1970s plastic grille.

As with the Bedford CF and Commer already mentioned, just about every converter of note used the Transit for transformation into a motorcaravan.

In 1965 a UK motoring legend was born – the Ford Transit replaced the Thames and changed the face of delivery vans forever. This cut-away picture clearly shows in detail all the many components that made up the new Transit. This particular model is a short-wheelbase van with twin opening rear doors, a model very popular with converters as the base for a panel van conversion with a rising roof.

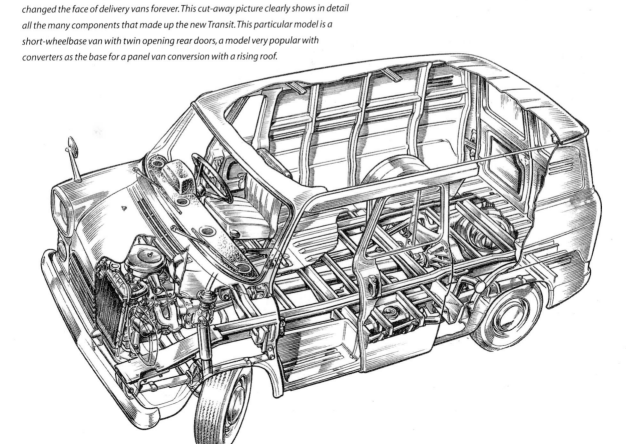

4 Auto-Sleeper

ABOVE: The Auto-Sleeper panel van layout was common to three base vehicles, the Bedford CF, Commer and Ford Transit. Pictured here is a MK I Transit that has been given a new paint finish.
RIGHT: Longevity within the world of motorcaravan manufacture is rare, certainly within the UK at least. Auto-Sleepers, based near Broadway, is an exception to the rule, having remained one of the country's top conversion outfits for approaching half a century. This family conversion of the BMC J2 is the model where it all began and from this conversion the new company was formed in 1961.

COMMER AUTO-SLEEPER

Auto-Sleepers of Willersey, Worcestershire, remains to this day the longest-running motorcaravan conversion specialist in the UK. From humble beginnings at their first factory near Cheltenham in 1960, the Trevelyan family began converting limited numbers of Austin 152/Morris J2 vans. From the outset these panel van conversions, with an ingenious rising roof, were all hand-built and very well designed. By early 1961 they had added the new Commer to their listing, but this had a slightly modified layout to that available on the BMC vans. Prices quoted in March 1961 were £889 for the BMC model and £895 for a Commer example.

Within a short period, the company dropped the conversions offered on the BMC J2 van to concentrate solely on the Commer conversion. Strangely, Auto-Sleepers offered no other conversion throughout the decade, remaining loyal to the Rootes/Chrysler Commer. In hindsight, though, it was the right choice, as its high-quality conversion based on this van deservedly earned the company an excellent reputation, both within the trade and with the motorcaravan buyers at the time. It was this reputation, combined with attention to detail, that would see the company (by now based at Willersey) go from strength to strength.

ABOVE: Initially Auto-Sleepers converted the BMC J2, but switched within a very short time to the Rootes Commer. For the remainder of the 1960s the company only offered its quality conversion on the Commer chassis. The first one is seen here; the Auto-Sleeper rising roof is beginning to take on a familiar shape. Note also on this very early Commer Auto-Sleeper that the side windows are top-hinged and open outwards. Later models would have sliding side windows and a GRP roof capping in white.

BELOW: Most panel van conversions are easily identified by the rising roof (in the raised position); the Auto-Sleeper has a definitive style and shape. This is an early Commer Auto-Sleeper with the front grille being an ideal feature by which to date it.

OPPOSITE PAGE:

TOP: The interior of a Commer Auto-Sleeper simply boasts quality workmanship from every crevice. It had the traditional layout of cupboards along each side with the seating/dinette area just behind the cab. The wooden trim on the dash fascia was a typical Auto-Sleeper trait; a wooden-hinged glove box was also added in place of the factory open shelf.
BOTTOM: Inside the Commer Auto-Sleeper looking back from the dinette area. The wardrobe is visible in the rear corner, with the sink unit positioned alongside it. The cooker and optional fridge were opposite. Also in this picture, note the addition of a vanity mirror on the inside of the roof side, just above the wardrobe.

THIS PAGE:

Auto-Sleepers made sure that no space went to waste within the interior, evident here with this shallow cupboard mounted on the rear door. With the door closed, the cupboard fitted perfectly into the recess at the side of the wardrobe, visible in the rear of the camper.

The Commer Auto-Sleeper had a very simple internal layout. When opening the rear doors one was confronted by a very usable floor space running from rear to front with furniture arranged along both interior sides of the van. Directly behind the cab seats was a dinette area, which could quickly be converted into a transverse double bed. These seats could also transform into two forward-facing seats. The high quality of the cabinet work was due to the fact that all the furniture was hand-built in-house by craftsmen. Mr Trevelyan had obviously studied the opposition's designs carefully and then improved upon them by packing a quart into a pint pot.

The kitchen area at the rear was very well equipped. It featured a two-burner gas hob with grill, a large sink and drainer, together with pumped water supplied from a 16gal (73ltr) under-floor tank. A refrigerator was available at extra cost. In and around the kitchen area was an array of storage cupboards and drawers, not to mention an ample amount of worktop space (these work-tops lifted to reveal the sink and cook-er). Even the inside of the twin rear doors was not neglected, as fixed here were cupboards with doors giving even more storage space.

One of the unmistakable trademarks of any Auto-Sleeper panel van conver-sion must be the patented elevating roof. This was a solid-sided, spring-assisted roof, which was simplicity itself to operate. The whole device could be quickly raised with two handles and locked in position; two side panels (incorporating windows) could then be lifted up very simply to form a neat and compact area, allowing full standing height. This very simple, and yet extremely clever roof system, first designed in 1960, is still offered today by Auto-Sleepers on the VW Trooper model.

The Commer Auto-Sleeper could sleep two adults in the transverse bed and gave the option of a double child's bed within the driving cab. In addition, bunks were available as an option for the space within the elevating roof, the conversion therefore being a six-berth model in total.

The company prided itself on the fact that so much equipment was packed into the conversion as standard, that it didn't need to offer that much in the way of optional extras. On the Commer conversion (using the year 1972 as an example) the fridge would have been an extra £35, underfloor gas cylinders £5, cab insulation £18, a tent/annex £56 and de luxe seats within the cab would have set you back an extra £31. According to the number of berths (and seats) required, the conversions on the Commer were given various designations: they were C20 (two-berth, seven seats); C21 (four-berth, seven seats); C22 (two-berth, six seats); C23 (as C22 but with a wide bed); and C24 (six seats and extra large double bed). The average price for a Commer Auto-Sleeper (in 1972) would have been around £1,350.

The company, as previously stated, remained very loyal to the Commer marque during its long production run. Auto-Sleepers continued to offer its conversion on this base when the vehicle became the Dodge-Spacevan and until it ceased production in the early 1980s. Because of this fact, a large number of Commer Auto-Sleeper models have survived to this day.

BEDFORD CF AUTO-SLEEPER

The company first broke with the tradition of only offering conversions on the Commer in the early 1970s. The Bedford CF became its first new model for a decade, though there was to be no innovative new design on the Bedford base; instead the company stayed with the tried and trusted layout that had proved so popular on the Commer conversion. Upon opening the twin rear doors of the Bedford one was met by almost a carbon copy of the Commer layout. Due to the tremendous following that the Bedford marque had gained over the years, the CF Auto-Sleeper very quickly established itself as a favourite with buyers. Initial Bedford models were based on the CF18 with the 1759cc petrol engine; the 22cwt model was soon added with the more familiar 2.3ltr petrol engine. The

This beautifully restored Bedford CF Auto-Sleeper carries the painted graphic 'Saved from the grave', as the owners did literally rescue it from the crusher. As the camper required so much work the couple saw it as an ideal opportunity to personalize the Bedford, adding alloy wheels, two-tone paintwork and chrome mirrors. The Auto-Sleeper roof was also removed and completely rebuilt.

OPPOSITE PAGE:

TOP LEFT: Be in no doubt, those 1960 and '70s Auto-Sleeper interiors really were in a class of their own. The delightful cabinetwork can be seen here on the unit housing the cooker and fridge. Also just visible in the corner, near the seat base, is a gas tap. This allowed for the use of a free-standing gas fire for chilly evenings.

TOP RIGHT: This is the cooker unit in use. The worktop lifts to reveal the gas hob, while metal flaps lift from each side to contain the heat. The wooden panel in the centre pulled down to give access to the gas grill. The three-pin electrical socket, seen on the end of the seat base, is a later addition common on many classic campers in order to obtain mains electricity when on campsites.

BOTTOM LEFT: Auto-Sleepers even fitted a lock with a key to the wardrobe, not a detail found in many conversions. The twin cupboard doors on the sink unit gave access to further storage. Recessed into the floor in front of this cupboard is the foot-operated water pump, which supplied water to the sink.

BOTTOM RIGHT: Interior shot of the Bedford CF Auto-Sleeper as viewed through the rear doors. The one benefit that the CF conversion had over the Commer model was the access from the living area to the driving cab. The engine on the Commer was situated between the cab seats, making access slightly awkward. The two side-facing seats seen here could be altered to give two forward-facing seats if required.

When the MK II edition of the Ford Transit was released, Auto-Sleepers carried over its familiar layout. As with the Bedford and Commer models, the two-dinette seats could provide two forward-facing seats. No seat belts were fitted as standard in the rear of campers at this time by any of the converters.

average price of a standard CF-based Auto-Sleeper in 1975 was around £2,500. The list of optional extras had by now grown to include brake servo, steering lock, automatic transmission, chemical toilet, gas tap and fire, fly screens, carpet in the rear, roof rack and an electrical water pump in place of the foot-operated device.

The trusted layout offered on both the Bedford and Commer bases was also used in two other vehicles, notably the MK I and MK II Ford Transit (Auto-Sleepers produced very few of these) and the Leyland Sherpa released in 1975. The Sherpa-based model became a very big seller indeed. The conversion on this Leyland offering did differ very slightly to the standard layout, however. Because the Sherpa was not as wide as the Bedford, Commer or Transit, it was unable to accommodate a double transverse bed. Instead, the sleeping arrangements were altered slightly to give two full-length single beds, making use once more of the dinette seats and this time the two cab seats, which reclined to lay flat.

It may not have escaped your notice that all the conversions offered by Auto-Sleepers up to this point have been panel van motorcaravans with an elevating roof. This was to change in 1977, when after seventeen years of doing conversions, the company released its first coach-built example.

AUTO-SLEEPER BEDFORD CB22

Everything that the company had learnt from many years of conversion work was carried forward to its new coach-built model. Auto-Sleepers used such slogans as 'Five-star luxury on wheels' to describe its latest offering. In fact, the sales brochure for this model stated 'such a complete specification there are no optional extras', which really did say everything about the new CB22. There was certainly nothing innovative about the exterior styling; it was very square with a traditional Luton area above the cab, although the roof of GRP manufacture was a one-piece system, therefore reducing the possibility of water leaks at a future date.

The CB22 was constructed using the established method of cladding a timber frame with aluminium panels, while the body – including the floor– was insulated with polystyrene throughout. For this model the company used the CF250 base with the 2279cc petrol engine fitted as standard; a GM 2064cc diesel was available as an option. The transmission was the familiar four-speed with floor-mounted gear change; the GM automatic box was another option available, together with an overdrive gearbox on the petrol engine.

Access to the coach-built living area was via a single rear door, with a folding access step incorporated below the entrance door. As with the Auto-Sleeper panel van conversions, the layout was similar but on a grander scale; in addition, a toilet/shower cubicle was fitted into the coach-built proportions. The furniture was placed once more along each internal wall, although this time a fridge was fitted as standard, as was a full cooker with oven. Another feature that was added to this model was the gas boiler for supplying hot

This was the first coach-built model that Auto-Sleepers released, the Bedford CB22, based on the CF chassis. It was an instant hit with the buyers – yet more Auto-Sleeper quality, but on a much larger scale! The CB22 remains a very popular model on the classic scene.

water to both the sink and the shower. Two other additions that could not be found in panel van models was a full cocktail cabinet with glasses and a floor-mounted gas fire.

Because of the coach-built dimensions of this model, it was possible to provide full double beds. One was made by the conventional method of using the dinette seats, while the other was to be found in the large Luton area above the cab, with access via a ladder. Just some of the other features found in the CB22 – and fitted as standard – were fly screens to all windows, three opening roof vents, carpet throughout, five fluorescent lights, vented locker (housing the gas cylinder), mains electrical socket, full complement of crockery and glass for four people, and a large wardrobe. It really was a most impressive list of standard features.

The interior of the coach-built CB22 was well designed and very spacious – it was advertised as 'Five star luxury on wheels'. It was so well equipped as standard that no optional extras were offered. It featured a toilet/shower, hot water heater, fridge, cooker, cocktail cabinet, full crockery set and bags of storage space.

5

Bariban

ABOVE: The Mercedes Ultra Autobahn by Bariban was often referred to simply as the Mercedes Bariban. Based on the 206D Mercedes with diesel power unit, the Ultra Autobahn was a luxury panel van conversion by Bariban of Devon. Occupants could enjoy standing room within the interior due to the GRP high-top roof. This model had both rear and side entry doors.

BARIBAN-MERCEDES
ULTRA AUTOBAHN

Motorcaravans today built on the Mercedes base vehicles are a common sight, but that was not the case back in the 1970s. The Bariban Company based in Newton Abbot, Devon, employed the

services of ex-Dormobile designer Bob Jones; the company had already enjoyed some success with its Freedom conversion, which was built for the northern distributors Madisons.

The Ultra Autobahn on the Mercedes 206D van required a conversion befitting such a prestige marque; the end

This side view of the Ultra Autobahn shows quite clearly the entrance doors available. Both side and rear doors were one-piece. The Mercedes 206D was a rather long, narrow vehicle and was in fact more popular as both a camper and delivery van on the continent than in the UK.

result was more than impressive. Here was a motorcaravan bearing the famous Mercedes-Benz badge, which really was the height of luxury in the panel van market. The Autobahn was powered by the 2.2ltr OM 615 diesel engine (as previously used in Mercedes saloon cars). In fact, the official Autobahn sales brochure stated clearly that this motor-caravan was only 10in (25mm) longer than the S-class Mercedes saloon. The vehicle featured a four-speed gearbox with floor-mounted gear change.

The first important point to note about this model is that it was a high top, having been fitted with an eye-catching GRP extended roof, which incorporated a cab luggage rack (with reinforced base). This therefore allowed full standing height over the entire living space area aft of the cab. Access to the motorcaravan (in addition to the two cab doors) was via a side-hinged door and a single (upward opening) tailgate. The layout was quite traditional, with

RIGHT: Interior plan of the Mercedes Ultra Autobahn.

BELOW: This Mercedes 206 model has been treated to an interior makeover at some point. The seat to the left in this picture could be altered to face forwards for travelling. Note also just how narrow the centre aisle of the interior is.

1. Side door
2. Single seat units with storage under
3. Clip-on dining table
4. Double seat units with storage under
5. Cocktail cabinet at eye level
6. Grocery cabinet at eye level
7. Water heater with fridge under
8. Rear access step
9. Rear tailgate
10. Wardrobe with cupboard over
11. Grill hob with oven and crockery cupboard under
12. Stainless steel sink unit with storage under

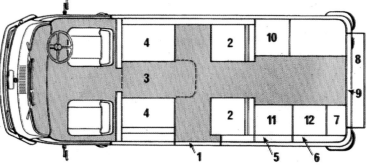

13. Convector fire below wardrobe
14. Pop-up side table
15. Shower area with hinged door, curtain, toilet and hand basin
16. Double/single bed layout with bunks over

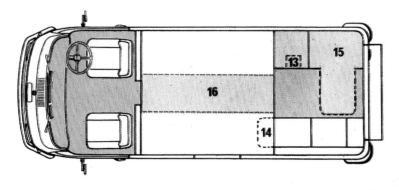

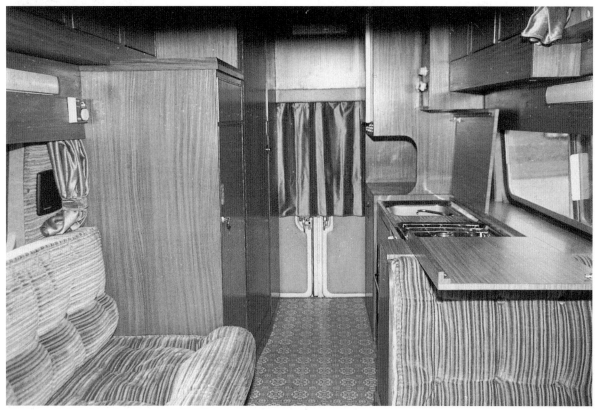

TOP: *Bariban offered its conversions from the early 1970s through to the early 1980s, moving from the original Mercedes 206D through various Mercedes models. Seen here is a Bariban dating from 1978, the Autobahn 305. The majority of Bariban panel van conversions featured high-top roofs; this is a rare rising-roof example leaving the factory.*

ABOVE: *Bariban used the design skills of former Dormobile designer Bob Jones and the company did deviate from the Mercedes offerings on occasions. Seen here is the interior of a Bariban Fiat Daily model from 1979. In fact, the interior layout is extremely similar to that of the earlier Ultra Autobahn.*

ABOVE: This particular Bariban model will be familiar to VW enthusiasts. Based on the bay model, this Palomino was fitted with a very distinctive roof that incorporated a roof rack at the front end.

RIGHT: A real rarity on the classic camper scene, the Commer Bariban. It is a model I have yet to see 'in the flesh', but the company obviously built one, as here is the proof. Judging by this press picture of the interior, it was finished to the usual very high standard.

furniture and kitchen along each side and a centre aisle leading to a dinette area just behind the cab seats. The kitchen was well appointed with a fridge and full cooker, with oven, as standard. A stainless-steel sink and drainer were positioned alongside the hob; a gas water heater supplied hot water to both the sink and shower. Both sink and cooker were hidden from view when not in use by means of lifting worktops. An additional lift-up worktop was placed next to the cooker to provide extra space when dishing up meals.

This model could seat up to ten adults, but only sleep four. In the living area the dinette seats would convert to either two long single beds or one double.

Within the GRP high top were two concealed bunks, which would accommodate another two people. Towards the rear of the vehicle was a well-appointed washroom with a shower, toilet and wash hand basin. The doors of the washroom would swing out to form a privacy screen. Other standard features included hard-wearing vinyl flooring, curtains to all windows and three fluorescent lights. All interior furniture was manufactured from real wood, with African hardwood mouldings, and black kickplates were fitted to all furniture bases to avoid marking.

The Bariban Company went on to convert later Mercedes models through the 1970s. In addition, they carried out

conversions on the VW LT model, the VW van (bay window) and a small number on the Commer base. The company would cease trading in 1979, having carried out some very attractive conversions. Their two most memorable models were without doubt the Ultra Autobahn featured here and the VW Palomino. Cost of the Mercedes Ultra Autobahn when new in 1974–75 was a fraction over £4,300. Readers may query the fact that I have listed model names throughout this book (in alphabetical order) and yet with this particular model I have listed the maker's name – the reason is that everyone (including tradespeople) commonly referred to this model as the Bariban Mercedes 206.

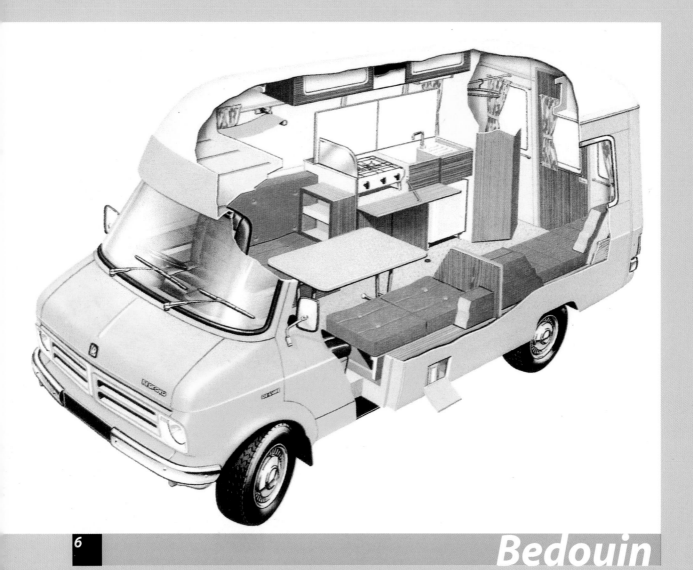

6

Bedouin

This cut-away diagram of the Bedouin gives a clear indication of all the features contained within. This model had a single rear door entrance and a combined toilet/wardrobe in the rear corner. Sink and cooker were positioned alongside the wardrobe, with a long settee opposite. This settee converted into a double bed, as did the dinette seats behind the cab. Internal furnishings, curtains and upholstery were typical of 1970s style and design, with bright orange and yellow being the theme.

BEDOUIN – BEDFORD CF

The Bedouin was a coach-built model released in 1970 by the giant CI/Motorized converters of Poole, Dorset. At the time of the Bedouin's release, CI/M, together with Dormobile of Folkestone, were the largest converters of motorcaravans in the UK. CI/M was already producing two coach-built models at the time – the highly successful Commer Highwayman and the Transit Sprite Motorhome.

The Bedouin was to be the third coach-built option within the company's range. Based on the CF 22cwt chassis cab with the deluxe cab, the entrance to the living area was via a rear entry single door. In external appearance it wasn't too dissimilar to the Commer High-

wayman, and was built using a very similar method of construction (aluminium panels over a wooden framework). The interior finish was also similar to that of the Highwayman, with wood-effect surfaces, the dinette converting to a double bed and the long seat near the rear also converting into an extra bed.

Upon entering the Bedouin from the rear door, a full-length wardrobe was positioned at the right rear corner with the kitchen facilities running alongside this. The kitchen featured a sink with draining board, a two-burner cooker with grill, optional fridge and storage cupboards, both at eye level, and beneath this the cooker unit. Covering both the cooker and sink was a split-worktop, allowing either the cooker or sink to remain concealed at any one

time. When both worktops were raised, the only food preparation surface available was the fold-down flap, which concealed the grill. When the optional fridge was purchased, this was positioned under the sink unit. Water was supplied to the kitchen sink via an electric pump, from a 16gal (73ltr) underfloor tank.

On the opposite side to the kitchen was a long upholstered seat, ideal for daytime lounging, which would then convert to a double bed in the evening. Beneath this was a large storage area. Forward of both these side-mounted features was the dinette area, which again had upholstered seating and a free-standing table; this area converted to another double bed with further storage beneath. These dinette seats could also be transformed into two forward-facing seats, although without the addition of seat belts/lap restraints at this time. Above the driving cab in the Luton area was additional storage space. Fitted above the dinette was a transverse rollaway bunk, which was rolled up and held with straps below the Luton area when not in use.

The living area of the Bedouin was double-skinned and fully insulated; ventilation was provided by an opening roof light and large sliding windows to each side. The three transistorized fluorescent strip lights, positioned at ceiling height, provided lighting.

Floor covering within the Bedouin was hard-wearing vinyl and brightly coloured curtains were fitted to all windows. The gas bottle was located beneath the floor and only accessible from the exterior. Optional extras on this model were very limited, consisting of a fridge, fly screen and sealed lid chemical toilet (this was housed at the base of the wardrobe).

Much to the annoyance of some buyers, the Bedouin was only available in one colour; this was a shade of sand/ gold (no doubt to match the Arabian model name of Bedouin). The whole of the roof area was painted in off-white.

The price for a Bedford Bedouin when it was released in January 1970 was £1,458/5s.

It should be noted that the initial water tank on this model during early production was 12gal (55ltr), as opposed to the later 16gal (73ltr), and the electric water pump was also a later addition – early models had a foot-operated pump. One point worth mentioning in relation to the Bedouin was the fact that it was the first coach-built model ever released by CI/Motorized on a Bedford. Previously, the company had only used BMC, Commer and Ford Transit bases for coach-built models. A

ABOVE: The Bedford CF Bedouin by CI Autohomes was only available in one colour, and this is it. Not an easy colour to describe, a sort of cross between English mustard and gold, in fact it was meant to resemble a shade of desert sand in order to tie in with the model name of Bedouin. The base vehicle was the 22cwt chassis with the coach-built section of aluminium panels over a timber frame; the entire body shell was insulated with glass-fibre wool.

RIGHT: On view here is the unit positioned alongside the wardrobe/toilet. This housed the combined sink/drainer, with cooker and grill below. Cupboards below these fitments were shelved for storage. Worktops have been lifted in this picture; they act as splashbacks for sink and cooker. The finish of cupboards within the Bedouin was a wood-effect laminate, seen here on the sink/cooker unit.

ABOVE: The free-standing table was placed between the inward-facing seats for dining. Because the table was of a free-standing design it could also be used outside, unlike many designs of the period (which clipped to brackets behind the cab seats and only had a support leg at the end). Note that the owner of this particular Bedouin has had the original seating reupholstered, with matching cab seats.

This is the view to the rear of the vehicle, from the dinette area. The single entrance rear door is clearly visible. To the right of the picture is the long settee, with backrest, which converted into a double bed. The base of the settee pulled out and was supported on three metal legs, two of which are just visible in the picture.

The long settee transformed into a double bed with the aid of the backrest. Even with two beds in use, there was still some free floor area in front of the sink/cooker unit. The door of the wardrobe/toilet was of the bifold design (hinged down the centre), so access to the toilet was also possible with both beds laid flat.

ABOVE: This picture shows the dinette seats converted into a double bed; occupants would sleep transversely across the camper. Just above this double bed, a stretcher bunk could be fitted by use of metal poles. This made the Bedouin a five-berth model.
RIGHT: The owner of this Bedouin obviously opted for a different paint finish to the standard colour. Modern wheel trims have also been added to give the Bedouin a more updated look.

little over halfway through the decade, the Bedouin was deleted from the catalogue, although the model name would reappear some years later.

Some months after the Bedouin was released, Wilson's, the motorcaravan dealers in London, offered a modified version of the Bedouin, which was given the title Wilson's Bedouin Executive GT. The modifications and extras added nearly £500 to the list price quoted by CI/Motorized. The modifications that were made by Wilson's included heavily tinted black windows (not in the cab area), power brakes, carpet, push-button radio, eight-track stereo system (or portable TV option) and a GT engine conversion. A fridge was fitted as standard to the Executive GT model, together with a fire extinguisher. The GT engine conversion was simply the addition of a twin-choke Weber carburettor, a higher compression ratio and revised air induction. One of the most notable external differences between the standard model and the Executive GT was the matt black front grille and headlamp surrounds; these were all colour-coded on the standard model.

7

Brigand

The Bedford CF Brigand was first released when the Poole-based company was still CI/Motorized, prior to becoming CI/M (CI Autohomes). This was a panel van conversion of the Bedford 18cwt van, although the 22cwt base could be ordered at extra cost. The Brigand was fitted with the Parkstone rising roof, unique to CI/M (CI Autohomes). This roof was also fitted to the company's Commer Wanderer and Transit Wayfarer panel van conversions.

BRIGAND-BEDFORD CF

The Brigand was the first motorcaravan to be released by CI/M based on a Bedford. It was unveiled in 1969 to be sold alongside the company's other popular panel van conversion, the Commer Wanderer. Both models featured the Parkstone rising roof and similar construction materials and interior styling.

The standard base for the Brigand was the 18cwt Bedford CF with the 22cwt base available as an option, with both benefiting from servo-assisted brakes. The Brigand had the familiar panel van interior layout – kitchen to one side and cupboards to the opposite side with the dinette converting to a double bed. This is the layout that had been employed by designers of panel van models (with rear doors) since the 1950s. It is straightforward, allows for a central aisle in the

middle of the van, and provides dinette seating that can quickly be converted into a double bed. The Brigand was advertised as a four-berth model for four adults, but in reality the two bunks within the Parkstone rising roof would be more comfortable for two children as opposed to adults. Access to bunks within a panel van conversion of this period was not easy, no matter which company carried out the conversion or how well designed it may have been.

Opening the rear doors of the Brigand would reveal the kitchen units along the right-hand side, with storage cupboards opposite. Kitchen facilities were the usual two-burner cooker with grill and alongside that the integrated sink/drainer. The whole of the space beneath the cooker and sink was storage, as the optional fridge on this model would be fitted into a cupboard on the opposite

side. The worktop on the Brigand kitchen was both split and bifold. The split system allowed either the cooker or sink to be concealed at any one time, while the bifold design meant that the worktop was double-folding from front to rear; this formed a splashback for the sink and/or cooker. Fresh water was electrically pumped from an underfloor tank to the sink, operated from a floor-mounted switch. Opposite the kitchen area was a range of cupboards, including a short wardrobe. Two drawers were also incorporated for yet more storage. The central cupboard here was vastly reduced in size if the optional fridge was ordered. Fully upholstered seating in the dinette converted into a double bed and two forward-facing seats for travelling. As is usual with this type of layout, the area beneath the dinette seats gave further storage space. The designers

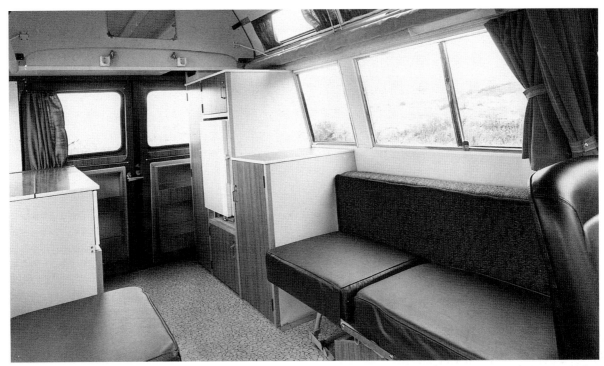

An interior press release picture of the Brigand model. Typical of panel van layouts during this period, it featured a dinette/double bed just behind the cab seats, with cooker, sink, fridge and wardrobe towards the rear. The insides of the twin opening rear doors were fitted with further storage pockets.

A cutaway diagram illustrating the internal features of the Brigand; note that the inward-facing dinette seats could be altered to make two forward-facing seats for travelling. Common practice on many CI/M models was the free-standing dining table, which could also be used outside. In addition to the lower double bed, the Brigand also had two rollaway stretcher bunks; these are coloured yellow in this picture.

had also utilized the inside of the rear doors by fitting open slimline shelving.

Storage of the gas bottle on this model was facilitated within a locker at floor level, inside the living area. The side windows on the Brigand were of the sliding design to aid ventilation and benefited from polished alloy frames. The window on the kitchen side of the vehicle ran the length of the living area, up to the rear of the cab. On the opposite side, however, the window was much smaller and situated to the area by the dinette. The original metal panel to the rear was left in place in order to form the rear of the wardrobe and fridge-housing cupboard. The sides of the van were fully insulated with glass-fibre padding; the inner of the Parkstone rising roof was also insulated. Curtains were fitted to all windows and the floor covering was a hard-wearing vinyl. Lighting within the living area of the Brigand came from two fluorescent lights.

The majority of Brigand models were either light blue or all white in body colour, but other colour options were available throughout production. Prior to the introduction of VAT in 1973, the Brigand carried a price tag of around £1,700. It ceased production in the mid-1970s. By this time, CI/Motorized had become CI/Autohomes and had completely altered its construction technique for coach-built models, by then building the living box independently of the chassis in its workshop and mounting the completed unit onto the base vehicle.

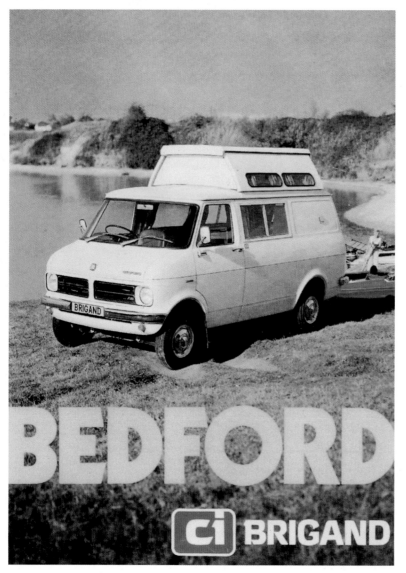

BEDFORD

CI BRIGAND

8

Calthorpe Home Cruiser

Bedford enthusiast Alan Kirtley lovingly restored this particular Bedford CA Calthorpe some years ago; it went on to win several awards at rallies and shows. Yet another example of a classic camper that was actually destined for the scrapyard but given a new lease of life by a classic vehicle fanatic.

CALTHORPE HOME CRUISER – THE FORD THAMES AND BEDFORD CA

In Chapter 1 I briefly mentioned the first post-World War II production motorcaravan released by Maurice Calthorpe early in 1957. Although a coach-built model, it still featured the Calthorpe rising roof, the first roof of its kind in the UK to be fitted to a motorcaravan. However, that first vehicle by Maurice Calthorpe is believed to have sold in very few numbers, so it was quickly deleted and replaced by a more conventional panel van conversion, again on the Bedford CA and once again featuring the Calthorpe rising roof. This model proved to be far more popular with buyers and sold in greater numbers. This panel van conversion is featured here.

Maurice Calthorpe will be best remembered within motorcaravanning

Bedford CA Home Cruiser as viewed through the twin rear doors. All essential fixtures such as cooker and sink are located along the left-hand side. The dinette/double bed is located opposite the cupboards and the bench seat, visible in the cab, folded down to create yet another double bed. There was also a stretcher bunk housed in the rising roof (more suitable for a child).

Calthorpe press photograph dating from 1962 showing the Thames Home Cruiser, with the roof in the raised position. In this year, the complete Calthorpe Home Cruiser range consisted of: Bedford CA, BMC J4, Commer, Ford Thames and Standard Atlas. All of these models were fitted with the arched Calthorpe rising roof.

A nicely restored Ford Thames Home Cruiser, this is a 1962 model based on the 400E chassis and fitted with a 1703cc petrol engine. All furniture, cooker and sink are positioned on the right-hand side of the Thames interior, with the settee opposite. This settee also acted as the double bed when the base was pulled out to extend it.

history as the man who designed and patented the first UK rising roof. In addition to this achievement, one should not overlook his excellent designs with regard to interiors. The Home Cruiser range was very well received from the outset in the 1950s. Models were available on several chassis throughout production including the Austin 152, BMC J4, Bedford CA, Commer, Ford Thames and Standard Atlas. I will focus on two of the Calthorpe Home Cruiser models within this chapter, the Bedford CA and the Ford Thames.

Conversions on the Ford Thames were based on both the 10/12cwt or 15cwt chassis, depending on customer requirements. The Thames Home Cruiser differed from conventional layouts of the period. Fitments within the interior were not located along each side of the van, the sides being reserved for long seats with a very narrow centre aisle. These well-upholstered seats were a great design feat, as not only would they fold up against the sides of the vehicle to give extra floor space, they could also be quickly converted into four bunk-style

berths. Within minutes, the seat backrests became the upper bunks, with legs unfolded from beneath them for support. The main cupboard and kitchen area in this model was located directly behind the cab seats, in the bulkhead position. In opting for this positioning of the kitchen, it meant that there was no access between the cab and the living area – one had to leave the cab and enter through the rear doors. This cupboard unit in light oak wood with mahogany edging housed a small sink, a two-burner hob and grill and storage cupboards. There was further storage at roof level, directly above this unit, again finished in light oak and featuring sliding doors. Positioned at each side of the kitchen unit, and running from floor level to roof height (with rising roof in the down position) were two narrow wardrobes. With the Calthorpe roof raised and beds in position for sleeping, there was still ample floor space for access to both the rear doors and the kitchen unit.

For ventilation, there were windows in both the vehicle sides and in the rising roof. Lighting within the interior was

supplied from a 12V lamp and gaslight; curtains were fitted as standard to all windows. For the purpose of dining, a free-standing wooden table was provided, allowing four people to eat in comfort; this table could also be used outside with the addition of camping chairs (not provided). Flooring within the vehicle was a vinyl covering. A water porter was provided as standard equipment for filling up the sink. The Ford Thames Calthorpe Home Cruiser, as exhibited at the 1960 Earls Court Motor Show, was being offered at a price of £845.

The Home Cruiser conversion on the Bedford CA base vehicle had the more familiar interior layout that was so popular on panel van conversions of the period. Upon entering the rear of the Bedford through the double doors there was a long upholstered seat running the length of the van on the right-hand side. This seat was certainly multifunctional; it could form a seating divan for four people, a dinette (with table) again for four and a single bed in the evening. When pulled down and out, it would also transform into a full double

The Calthorpe Home Cruiser stand at the 1961 Earls Court Motor Show, Commer in the foreground and Standard Atlas to the left. The BMC J4 can be seen to the right of the Commer, with the Bedford CA example at the rear.

bed. Along the left-hand side was the kitchen and wardrobe. As with the Ford Thames model, the cabinetwork was in light oak with mahogany trim. The kitchen contained a sink, two-burner cooker with grill and storage cupboards beneath. The wardrobe was situated next to the kitchen in the left-hand corner of the vehicle.

A Home Cruiser based on the Bedford was available on both the 10/12cwt or 15cwt base vehicle and one clever use of space on the Bedford was the alteration of the front bench seat in the cab. This bench seat could be reversed to face the interior living space, thus providing seating for six people when combined with the standard seat, which ran the length of the Bedford. This design feature was significant within the realms of motorcaravan history and development. Calthorpe and, earlier, Martin Walter Ltd (Dormobile) both installed this seating arrangement, which allowed the driving compartment to form part of the interior living space. Despite the advantages of this seating system very few converters followed the trend. The irony of this is

that nearly all modern motorcaravans (panel van and coach-built models) feature cab seats which swivel around to form part of the living space. The front bench seat in the Bedford could also be arranged to lie flat and provide another double bed (in addition to the rear one).

Floor covering in the Bedford was vinyl and curtains were supplied for all windows. Interior lighting was supplied from both 12V electrics and gas. Water to the kitchen sink was delivered via a hand pump, drawn from a water porter situated in the cupboard below. The Bedford, of course, had the patented Calthorpe rising roof fitted as standard. The cost of a Bedford Home Cruiser in 1960 would have been around £820, depending on which base option was specified. The registered office for M. Calthorpe (Home Cruiser) Ltd was Park Lane (later Oxford Street), London, but these certainly were not the factory addresses. The coachbuilders F. Stuart & Son Ltd built many Home Cruiser models in Shepperton, while Home Cruiser Coachworks Ltd of Walton-on-Thames, Surrey, built later models.

Today we are all well aware that a motorcaravan can have a variety of uses, but during the infancy of this leisure activity the designers, coach-builders and indeed advertisers were trying extremely hard to get these points across to potential buyers. This is how the Calthorpe Home Cruiser sales brochure sung the praises of its product in the late 1950s:

With a Calthorpe 'Home Cruiser' the world is yours – smart resorts – beautiful country – woodlands – mountain resorts and gay cities – places which were only a distant hope are now attainable at a fraction of the cost, with none of the usual troubles of booking hotel accommodation, packing, unpacking, etc., and the inevitable bills and tipping. You simply hang your clothes in the wardrobe, place your travelling necessities in the spacious lockers and drive wherever you wish, completely independent and free of tiresome and often expensive accommodation arrangements.

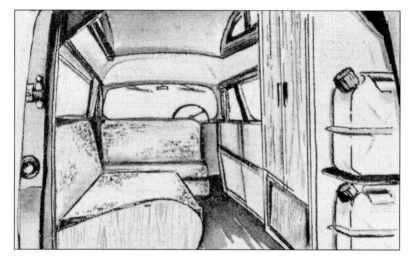

Artist's impression of the Bedford CA Home Cruiser interior. This clearly indicates slight detail design changes during production of the Home Cruiser range. The earlier photograph of the restored Bedford shows the furniture on the opposite side. The Calthorpe brochure for 1962 closely follows this drawing, as the floor plan published is identical.

Commer Home Cruiser circa 1962. This picture is ideal for studying the very early front panel of the Rootes Commer. Note that the individual chrome 'COMMER' letters had not yet appeared; instead there was a pressed badge fitted just below the front waistline. Another interesting detail is the three chrome trim strips below the badge; an air intake/grille had not been added at this time.

Interior press release photograph of the Commer Home Cruiser. Both cooker and sink are seen on the left, with worktops raised. The wardrobe was in the left rear corner and the settee was opposite. The bench seat in the foreground could be turned over to face the rear for dining. This picture also shows the inside of the Calthorpe roof very nicely. The centre windows within the raised roof were of the sliding variety; all others were fixed in position.

9

Canterbury Savannah

Canterbury-Pitt launched the Ford Transit Savannah at the 1967 Geneva Motor Show. At this point, Canterbury was still producing models under licence from Peter Pitt. This 1968 press picture illustrates that the early Savannah models were pure Peter Pitt ingenuity. Peter's open-plan layout was still being used, with both the cooker and tip-up sink fixed to the insides of the rear doors.

CANTERBURY SAVANNAH – FORD TRANSIT

The Canterbury Savannah was based on the MK I Ford Transit and was first unveiled at the Geneva Motor Show in 1967. The conversion was carried out on the 1.7ltr (petrol) 90 Custom chassis. This early release was in fact built at a time when the official name of the company was still Canterbury-Pitt. The MK I Savannah featured double-opening rear doors, on the insides of which were fitted the sink and cooker. The interior was also the standard Peter Pitt open-plan layout. Canterbury had reached agreement with Peter Pitt in the early 1960s to use his designs under licence; part of that agreement was that the Pitt name would feature in

the title of the company producing motorcaravans.

When Peter passed away in 1969 that licensing agreement came to an end and the company reappeared as Canterbury Industrial Products (Aveley) Ltd, based in Basildon, Essex. The Savannah model had by this time been redesigned but given the title Savannah MK II. It was still a panel van conversion with a fabric rising roof, but in place of the double-opening rear doors was a one-piece door which lifted up. Canterbury offered an optional rear awning/tent which could be fitted tightly to the rear of the vehicle and allow the one-piece rear door to remain open. The Savannah was in production for a number of years and ran from the initial MK I through to the MK

IV. Focus in this chapter will be on the MK II variation that was so popular during the early 1970s.

Looking inside the vehicle from the rear, with the one-piece door in the raised position, the conventional panel van layout was evident. To the right was the sink, housed within a cupboard/drawer unit, a further storage locker mounted on the wall, and in the right-hand corner was the fridge, fitted as standard on this model. On the opposite side to this was the two-burner cooker with grill and a wardrobe housed in the rear left-hand corner. The dinette, situated behind the cab seats, consisted of two facing seats with back support cushions and a free-standing table. The seats converted into a double bed and there were two additional

ABOVE: By 1974 the Pitt name had been dropped from the model title; it was now the Canterbury Savannah. This picture shows the MK III model, when the sink/cooker had been moved to a more traditional position inside. The twin rear doors had also given way to a lifting tailgate. Although the basic roof design remained the same, side windows had by this time been incorporated into the side canvas.

RIGHT: Interior of the Savannah MK III with the dining table in position. This model featured the traditional layout of inward-facing dinette seats that converted into a double bed.

beds, of the rollaway bunk variety, housed within the rising roof. There was an option of a stretcher bunk, suitable for a child, within the driver's cab area.

The rising roof on the Savannah remained very familiar throughout its long production run. The main top cap-ping of this design was constructed of insulated GRP and had an amber sky-light together with two vents. This was a huge rising roof, which covered the whole of the living area within the vehicle. The main frame of the roof was of metal construction and was clad with a red and white striped material. Other standard features of the MK II Savannah included carpet, fluorescent light, 6gal (27ltr) freshwater tank and a full complement of crockery and cutlery. A Canterbury Savannah in standard form carried a price tag of £1,400 at the height of its popularity in 1972. The rear tent/awning was an additional £45.

ABOVE: MK III Savannah arranged for sleeping. The dinette seating has been laid flat to form a double bed. Two stretcher bunks ran the length of the rising roof. No ladder was supplied; access to the bunks was via a 'leg up' from mum and dad!

Because the Savannah was in production for some years it can sometimes prove a little difficult to differentiate between early releases. To clarify, the model was originally released by Canterbury-Pitt in 1967. This initial model featured nearly all the Peter Pitt design characteristics of his open-plan layout, including door-mounted cooker and sink. There then followed a MK I facelift model, on which the twin rear doors were replaced by the one-piece tailgate. Because of this, the cooker and sink were moved into the vehicle and it began to resemble the MK II Savannah (this was done later in 1967). Although many surviving Savannah models may by this time have been repainted, the majority of them left the factory with a light blue exterior paint finish (with white as an option) and that distinctive GRP roof capping painted white. The two most distinguishable features of the Savannah models were the rising roof in the raised position and the one-piece rear tailgate. The Savannah was only ever available based on the Ford Transit.

Cutaway drawing of the Canterbury Savannah dating from 1973.

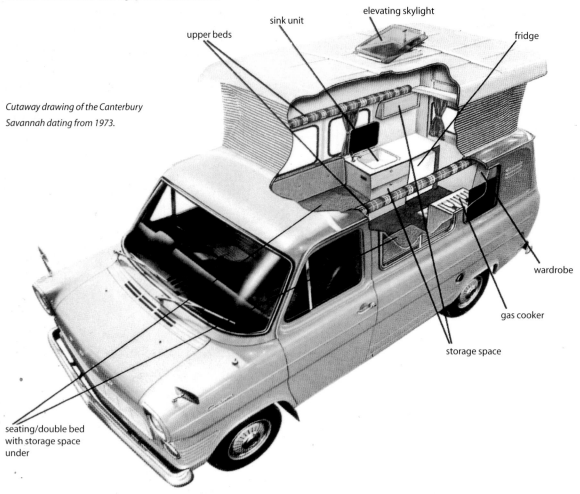

elevating skylight

sink unit

upper beds

fridge

wardrobe

gas cooker

storage space

seating/double bed with storage space under

10

Car-Camper

The Commer Car-Camper Series IIIB, circa 1967. The tiled floor was a distinctive trademark of the Car-Camper conversions. The traditional layout featured sink and cooker to the left, with chest of drawers and wardrobe opposite. Dinette seats converted into a double bed.

CAR-CAMPER – COMMER 1500

Auto Conversions of Birmingham produced the first Car-Camper models back in 1958, though at that time the base vehicle employed for conversion was the BMC J2. This was a quality panel van conversion of great craftsmanship and excellent design, which quickly earned the company a good reputation within the industry. When the Commer 1500 was released in 1960, both base vehicles were listed as an option for conversion, although it would be the Rootes

Commer that found more favour with the buyers.

The story of the Car-Camper Commer is divided between two models, the early release in 1960 with its front-hinged rising roof and the later model with a GRP roof featuring solid sides and end panels. But in spite of this roof difference, the interior finish and layout were pretty much standardized on both early releases and later models. Throughout production of the Car-camper Commer two layout options were available, the Series IIIA and the Series IIIB.

The only real difference between these two options was a very ingenious design feature, a ready-made double bed on the Series IIIA. Therefore the opening description given here of the Car-Camper Commer will remain the same for both model options until the description relating to the dinette/double bed.

With the twin rear doors open and locked into that position with the help of metal stays, the first piece of the interior to be noticeable was wooden cupboards secured to the interior of each rear door. These cupboards were of a

ABOVE: *This is the sink unit of the Car-Camper, situated immediately to the left when looking through the rear doors. It consisted of a combined plastic sink and drainer with hand pump. The worktop over the sink was a bifold design, seen here positioned as a shelf. The two-burner hob with grill is alongside the sink, with a one-piece worktop.*

LEFT: *Converters would make use of every available space within a van, the insides of rear van doors being a case in point. This is the unit on the inner rear door of the Commer Car-Camper, with built-in crockery holder.*

good size and had hinged fronts that dropped down to reveal storage for crockery and cups. Looking into the vehicle from the rear, there were wooden units to each side. On the right-hand side was a chest of drawers, with a good-sized wardrobe in the right-hand corner (on the early Commer conversions the cooker and sink were very often located on this side). If the optional fridge was specified, then two drawers of the three-drawer chest were lost in order to accommodate it. Opposite, on the left-hand side of the interior, were the sink/drainer and standard two-burner cooker with grill (an optional full oven was available). Beneath these pieces of equipment were cupboards, the one nearest the vehicle rear end housing a water carrier. A hand vacuum pump located next to the sink delivered water from the tank to the sink. Worktops covered both the sink and the cooker, lifting back to form splashbacks (on later models the worktop over the sink was hinged in the middle as well to form a useful shelf when secured with a simple bolt).

Series IIIA

Next we come to the dinette area and this is where the major change between the two models occurred. The Series IIIA featured a ready-made double bed housed within a raised, hidden section of the dinette floor. With this arrangement, the table and seat cushions were removed and the wooden seat structure folded flat. In turn, this structure was then lifted vertically to form a screen between the living area and the front cab. A 4in (100mm) Texofoam mattress remained on the floor during travelling when the seating structure was again lowered. Despite being a very clever and well-engineered design, this feature never did really grab the attention of buyers, who preferred the simplicity of the bed within the Series IIIB.

Series IIIB

The double bed on this model option was far more conventional in its design. The wooden Formica-topped table was placed on a ledge between the seats, which were then laid flat across both the seat bases and the table to form a double bed. There is probably a very

Interior of the Commer Car-Camper with the dinette being prepared as a double bed. The dining table was used to bridge the gap between the two seats, then the seats were folded flat over both the seat bases and the table.

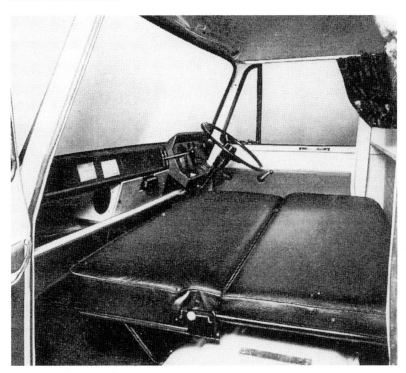

Both the Series IIIA and IIIB Car-Camper models had the option of a child's bed in the cab area. With this option a hinged bench seat replaced the standard factory seats. In addition to this bed, a further stretcher bunk could also be installed into holders that were positioned slightly higher than the steering wheel.

good reason why this model was more popular than the ready-made bed option of the Series IIIA. The seats in the cab area were of the bench variety (base and backrest), and on both model options these folded flat to form a three-quarter-width bed suitable for two children. Access to and from the cab

with the Series IIIA bed raised would have been impossible; hence the reason why the simplicity of the Series IIIB system proved far more popular with parents! Also available as an option on the Car-Camper Commer was an extra child's hammock-style bunk, which fitted into holding cups transversely just

Early Car-Camper models were based on the BMC J2, although the interior layout changed little over the years, even when applied to the Commer and Ford Transit. This cutaway drawing of the J2 shows the Series IIIA model with the ready-made double bed. Note that the floor area under the dinette is raised slightly, which is where the permanent bed was housed beneath a false floor.

The same Series IIIA model with the beds made up. Note here that the false floor has been lifted up to act as a wall between the cab and living area. This picture also shows the optional single bed, arranged lengthways over part of the double bed and the storage cupboard.

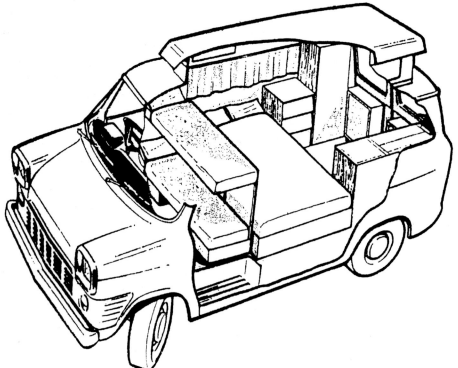

Interior of the Transit Car-Camper with beds made up. On the Transit model the beds in the driving cab were of the bunk variety. Apart from this detail, the remainder of the interior was very much as other models in the Car-Camper range.

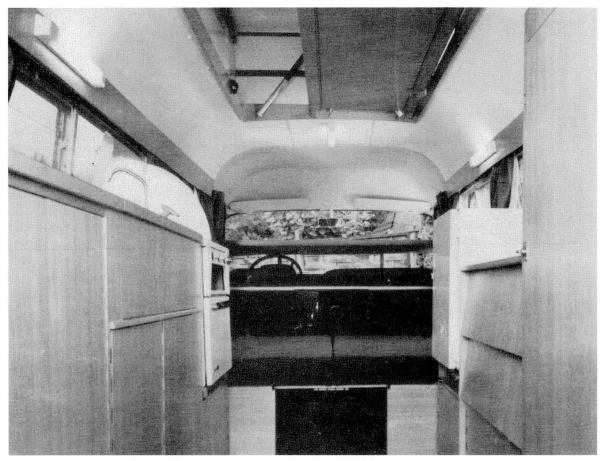

This happens to be the Transit model, but the aim of this picture is to illustrate the two main optional extras available within the Car-Camper interiors. On the right of the picture a fridge has been added next to the chest of drawers. On the Commer models the fridge would have been positioned in place of the chest of drawers (this is the long wheelbase Transit, thus it could house both a fridge and chest of drawers). Opposite the fridge a full cooker has been fitted in place of the standard two-burner hob and grill.

above steering-wheel height. When not in use, this bunk was rolled up and stored behind the cab seats.

Both the Series IIIA and IIIB were offered as Walkthru models, that is to say that an access gap was left in the wooden bulkhead to allow one to gain access to the cab and living area in the rear. Even with this option, though, access was somewhat limited as the engine on the Commer was positioned between the driver and passenger.

The early Car-Camper conversions were fitted with a front-hinged rising roof, similar in style to the German Westfalia roof seen on VW models. This was dropped in the early 1960s to be replaced by a Sherwood rising roof, constructed entirely of GRP. Two wooden handles were pushed upwards from inside the vehicle and the whole roof lifted by means of both piano hinges and runners. Early roofs of this type had non-opening windows incorporated into the sides; later models had small sliding windows. A lifting roof vent was fitted as standard to aid ventilation.

Another noticeable feature to change dramatically between early models and later releases was the vehicle side windows. The early conversions had separate small windows of the trailer caravan variety, which opened upwards from the bottom by use of top hinges. The later side window has opening louvres to each centre section, with fixed glass at either side. Curtains were fitted as standard to all vehicle windows, including the cab. Lighting within the Car-Camper Commer changed throughout production, with early examples having both gas and electric lighting, while later models were fitted with the commoner fluorescent lights. Gas bottles were carried in a cradle beneath the vehicle. Most Car-Campers had a tell-tale interior design trait, in that they were fitted with vinyl floor tiles, often in a combination of light grey with either blue, red or black. Some customers did, however, stipulate a one-colour vinyl in lieu of the tiles.

Auto Conversions later became Car Campers Limited, with the factory moving from Birmingham to nearby West Bromwich. The company continued to produce motorcaravans well into the 1990s, often on large Mercedes bases, having by then moved to premises in Barnstaple, Devon. Although the majority of Car-Campers from the classic period were based on the Commer 1500 and 2500 bases, the Ford Transit was also listed as an option. For a short period the company produced a micro-camper, based on the MK II Ford Escort van.

The prices of the various Commer options, using the year 1970 as an example, were: Series IIIA £1,140; Series IIIB £1,125; and Series IIIB Walkthru £1,147. A custom cab version on all models was available at an extra cost of £60 in 1970. This included a padded fascia panel, padded engine cover and wheel arches within the cab and a padded section to infill the panel below the front parcel shelves. Other optional extras were: Duotone paint finish; full oven; floor-mounted gas point (for a fire); chemical toilet; fridge; fly screens; roof rack; toilet tent; rear awning/tent; and full underbody underseal.

11

Coaster

Dormobile conversions can be found on a wide variety of base vehicles and as the Commer was so popular during the classic years, it was hardly surprising when a Commer Dormobile appeared. This is the Dormobile Coaster with that famous side-hinged roof. A Commer enthusiast has lovingly restored this model.

COASTER – COMMER

Martin Walter Ltd produced its first conversion on the 1500 Commer chassis in 1960, to coincide with the release of the new vehicle from the Rootes group. However, this particular model was not given the name Coaster, it was simply the Dormobile Caravan based on the Commer van, with side-loading door. This early model was typical Dormobile, featuring the well-tried Dormatic seating, the famous candy stripe rising roof and a wood-grain plastic finish to the furniture. The Dormobile Commer Caravan had twin rear doors, which opened to reveal a cooker and sink unit on the right-hand side, with a spacious wardrobe to the left. Alongside the wardrobe were 5gal (23ltr) and

2gal (9ltr) water tanks fitted with taps. The seats for dining, which converted into a double bed, were situated just behind the cab area. This model was available as both a four-berth and two-berth, with stretcher bunks contained within the large Dormobile roof.

In 1969 the Dormobile Caravan on the Commer was re-released as the all-new Dormobile Coaster. In fact, several publications at this time proclaimed that this was the first Dormobile to be built on the Commer van. Quite where these people had been hiding for the previous ten years I don't know! The Coaster was unveiled on the D. Turner stand at the 1969 COLEX (Camping and Outdoor Life and Travel Exhibition) show. D. Turner was in fact Derek Turner, owner of the SE London Motorized Caravan Centre, a

long-established supplier of motorcaravans in London and a well-respected supplier of all Dormobile models. The actual model on display on the D. Turner stand was in fact the prototype Coaster. Externally it looked very similar to the model first released by the company in 1960. Once again, it was fitted with the Dormobile rising roof and, as before, it was based on the Commer van with side-loading door. There was, however, one cosmetic change to the exterior bodywork of the new model, the famous Dormobile side flashing (a combination of aluminium trim running the length of the vehicle and in-filled with a contrasting body colour) was now missing on the new Coaster.

The interior of this new model bore little resemblance to the original

View through the side entry door of the Coaster. Kitchen facilities are immediately in front with work surfaces to the right. The double seat in the foreground has been arranged for dining, with the table in position. Curtains and seat upholstery are non-standard.

BELOW: Looking towards the cab area from the rear. Seats are again arranged for dining. The roof is in the raised position, with the two rolled-up stretcher bunks just visible.

Dormobile Commer. The designers this time opted to lay out the interior in a similar fashion to that on many VW campers, with the bed to the rear and slightly to one side, and all furniture positioned along the interior side. The transverse bed on most Commer campers utilized the dinette seats, which gave a bed length of exactly 6ft (1,829mm) across the van (as with models like the Auto-Sleeper and Car-

Camper). By positioning the bed of the Coaster to the rear, Dormobile managed to add an extra 4in (100mm) to the bed length. There was, however, a price to pay for fitting the bed at the rear, as it meant that large items could not be carried within the vehicle on a day to day basis when the vehicle wasn't being used for camping. For many people, the beauty of owning a panel van conversion is that it can be a multi-functional

vehicle, ideal as back-up during house moves and fetching long/large pieces of wood from the local DIY store. Placing the bed at the rear on a rear-engine van like the VW appears quite logical, but to do this on a front-engine van with twin rear doors, like the Commer had, made little commercial sense to my way of thinking. But used purely for camping purposes, the Coaster layout was more than acceptable.

Another view through the side-entry door of the Coaster, but this time with the double bench seat arranged for forward-facing travel.

The Coaster interior arranged for night-time. Lower seating has been converted into a double bed and the two stretcher bunks are in position within the Dormobile roof. With all beds in position it was still possible to reach that all-important kettle for a brew!

Seats within the rear of the Coaster arranged for travelling. All are forward-facing here, seating a total of five people. It will be noted that none of the seats was fitted with any type of seat belt or lap restraint; this was common practice during the classic years and in fact seat belts in the rear of campers were not common until the 1990s.

The rear of the Coaster with the dining table and seats in position around it. With the shorter bench seat in the foreground, this left ample room for the person using the kitchen facilities to manoeuvre.

Running along the vehicle interior, directly behind the driver's seat, was the main Coaster furniture. This consisted of units at waist height housing the gas cooker (two-burner hob with grill), plastic sink, cool box (a fridge was an optional extra) and wardrobe. Fresh water was kept in a 3gal (14ltr) plastic container beneath the sink and pumped up to the sink via a foot-operated pump. Provision for the storage of a gas cylinder was within a box just inside the rear doors. Storage was a big plus point on the Coaster, with shelving under both the cooker and sink. Below the drainer was a cutlery drawer. The rear wardrobe was of ample proportions and had a shallow shelf at the top. For the storage of bedding, there was more than enough room within the bench seat base.

The Coaster could seat four people for dining purposes and for travelling, although seven people could be seated in comfort. In addition to the rear double bed already mentioned, there were two stretcher bunks within the rising roof and the driving compartment could be converted to sleep two children. Lighting was provided via fluorescent strip lights. Curtains were supplied as standard for all windows. The flooring was a combination firstly of vinyl, then a removable carpet. From its conception in the mid-1950s the huge Dormobile rising roof was one of the biggest fitted to any panel van conversion, and certainly one of the best. The GRP capping of this roof was fitted with two windows and a couple of opening

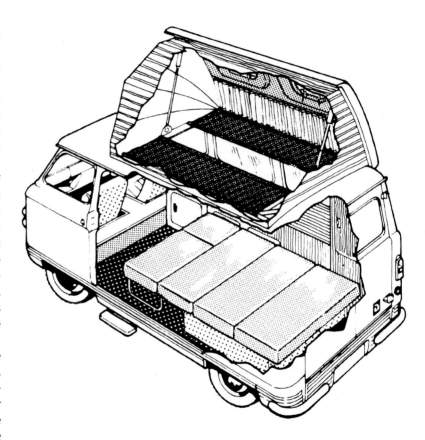

Cutaway drawing of the Commer Coaster by Dormobile. This particular drawing shows the camper arranged for sleeping, with the lower seats converted into a double bed and the two stretcher bunks in place within the roof space. The coaster was fitted with twin opening rear doors in addition to the side entry door.

air vents. To aid air circulation within the living area, two air-scoop Dormobile windows were incorporated into each side vehicle window. An interesting standard fitment on later Coaster models was a raised roof warning light. This was a dash-mounted light that would illuminate when the ignition was

switched on if you were about to drive away with the roof still up!

The cost of a Dormobile Coaster in 1972 would have been £1,377 in standard form. The cost of the original Dormobile Caravan on the Commer base, back in 1960, was £908 for the four-berth model.

12

Cotswold

On view here is the Cotswold Concorde based on the MK I Ford Transit. Mr Lucas, of the automotive electrical company, owned this particular vehicle from new. It contained a host of extras not usually included in the standard Concorde model and cost £11,000 back in 1971.

COTSWOLD – FORD TRANSIT CONCORDE

Kingscote and Stephens of Gloucester released the first Cotswold motor-caravan in early 1962. It was a unique panel van conversion on the BMC J2 minibus base and included both a rear and side entry door. The design feature that made this conversion so unusual was the fitted high top manufactured from GRP. It was a design that was simply years ahead of its time. Although such companies as Martin Walter Ltd, Cal-thorpe, Locomotors and Car-Campers had all used GRP for such items as body mouldings and roof capping, no con-verter had at that time produced a full high top on a panel van model. Sadly, the public simply didn't rush to buy this new innovation and it failed to sell in any quantity. However, as the decade unfolded, this company would enjoy

greater success with its well constructed coach-built models.

After the failure of its high-top panel van offering, the company switched its attention once more to the BMC J2, but this time it produced a superb, stream-lined coach-built example, which was given the title the Cotswold C-Series. This was a coach-build of traditional con-struction using aluminium sheets over a wooden framework. The entrance door to the living area was just to one side of the passenger cab door. It featured a rear U-shaped lounge/dinette, large kitchen area, which included a full oven, toilet cubicle and large wardrobe. All interior cabinetwork was finished in a wood-effect laminate; the rear panel near the lounge/dinette had a large window from which to observe the scenery whilst din-ing. It proved to be a very popular model within the Cotswold range and the C-Series was carried over to the BMC 250JU

when it was introduced in the late 1960s. Running alongside the C-Series was a slightly longer model, which was desig-nated the C-Series Major. The Major had more floor and cupboard space and also carried the option of having two single beds in place of the standard double. This model proved to be the forerunner to the luxury Concorde model of the 1970s Cotswold range. As the 1970s dawned, the company was trading as Ken Stephens Caravans Ltd, although still based in Gloucester.

The late 1960s through to the mid-1970s would prove to be the pinnacle of success for the Cotswold range (it disappeared after this time from all motorcaravan listings). By far the most successful model for the company proved to be the Concorde, which was available on the BMC 250JU, Ford Tran-sit and Mercedes Benz 408D. It sold in greater numbers based on the Ford

Front view of the large Transit Cotswold Concorde; just visible is the side entrance door. The front of this Transit has the bull-nose front end, which signifies that the engine is either 3ltr petrol or a diesel option.

The rear dinette area of a Concorde model with table in position. Because it was a side-entrance model, this allowed for the positioning of a large rear window in the back panel. This dinette converted into a double bed in the evening. Just seen to the right is the wardrobe with a large mirror on the door.

Transit 130 chassis and it is this model that will be the focus of this section. The overall design was similar to that of the initial C-Series on the BMC base. The entrance door to the living area was again on the side of the vehicle, slightly back from the passenger cab door; an entrance step folded down from the bodywork to aid access. Immediately to the left when inside the vehicle was the toilet/shower cubicle, which also had a fitted foldaway sink with a mirror above and a shaver point. The full-length door to the toilet/shower could be fixed to the side of the wardrobe opposite to allow for extra space when using the facilities (though it was a good idea to lock the side entrance door at this point!). On the left-hand side, when standing inside the entrance door, was the very large wardrobe; this contained a rail, hooks, top shelf and a big mirror. A flued gas heater was positioned at the base of the wardrobe front door.

Turning to the area behind the cab, a three-quarter-height door was located in the centre, adjacent to the toilet/shower. This allowed for access between the cab and living area. To the side of this door, and immediately behind the driver's seat, was the full cooker with oven. The kitchen was L-shaped and ran from this point around and along the inside of the vehicle interior. This was a very well equipped kitchen and consisted of a fridge, chest of drawers and stainless steel sink with drainer, together with pressurized hot and cold water. Running along the top of the

LEFT: When opening the side entrance door of the Concorde, one would have seen this view first upon entering. Full cooker, fridge and hot water heater were all housed within the spacious kitchen unit. The seat to the side in this shot was one of two seats just behind the cab. They acted as separate dining for two persons and also formed a bunk-style bed in the evening.

ABOVE: A real period feature of many older campers is the gas lamps. This stylish example was mounted on the wall to the side of the wardrobe. The curved metal section behind and on top was a safety feature to deflect heat away from the wood ceiling! They remain a usable period feature, but a degree of care does of course have to be taken, including the servicing of all gas appliances.

kitchen area were ceiling-height storage cupboards, one of which contained a full set of crockery as standard. Wood-effect laminate work surfaces covered the whole of the kitchen area, including the cooker. Those on both the sink/drainer and cooker lifted to act as splashbacks when these appliances were in use.

Moving towards the rear of the vehicle interior, and positioned on the side of the wardrobe, was a small cocktail cabinet that contained a set of sherry glasses and wine glasses. There was a conventional dinette at the rear with two upholstered seats facing inwards – four people could be comfortably seated here at meal times. A table clipped to the inner rear wall of the vehicle with a metal leg to one end for support, in line with all Concorde furniture. The table had a wood-effect laminate top. The dinette seating converted easily into a double bed. A specified option on the Concorde was the availability of two single beds in the dinette area, in place of the standard double. On both the bed options there was plenty of additional storage space within the bed bases.

All Cotswold models were very well equipped; the luxurious Concorde was no exception. This is the range of wall-mounted storage lockers situated over the kitchen. Cotswold used a light-grain wood-effect laminate finish to all its furniture.

A three-quarter-berth model was added to the Concorde options and this consisted of two single seats immediately behind both the driver and passenger cab seats (where the toilet/shower and cooker were placed on the two-berth model). A small table for dining was placed between the two single seats, in line with the access door between the cab and living area. At night these two single seats (with the aid of the table) formed a single bed and a stretcher bunk was placed above this to complete the four-berth option.

The Concorde had a light and airy feel to it, no doubt due to the well-placed windows around the vehicle. In addition to the standard cab windows, there was a large rear window, smaller single windows either side of the dinette, another window over the working area of the kitchen and a small window within the top of the main entrance door. There was a window of frosted finish in the toilet/shower cubicle, a small square window directly behind the driver's seat and a window in the top part of the dividing door between the cab and living area. In addition to all of this glazing, there was also a roof vent allowing stale air to escape. This vent had a fly screen fitted as standard, as did the three opening windows within the living area.

The whole of the coach-built body was fully insulated with glass-fibre.

Water storage on this model was ample for touring holidays – a 16gal (73ltr) tank for fresh water and a 6gal (27ltr) tank for hot water. Both hot and cold water were electrically pumped to the sink and shower. Lighting was also more than adequate, four fluorescent lights and one gas lamp being the standard fitment. Completing the interior fitments were curtains to all windows, fitted carpet and upholstery in a variety of colour options.

This was a luxury conversion and there was a price to pay – back in 1971 a Ford Transit Cotswold Concorde was listed at a touch over £3,000. The benefit of such a well-appointed motorcaravan was that there were few optional extras that required adding by the buyer. The Ford 2.0ltr V4 petrol engine as standard with manual transmission powered this model. Buyers could request a diesel engine for an extra £130 and/or automatic transmission for £94. However, the 2ltr petrol engine proved to be by no means powerful enough to pull this huge, heavy coach-built model, and many owners later added the bull-nose Transit front in order to accommodate either the 2.5ltr or 3.0ltr engine.

As noted above, the Concorde was available on other bases. The price of these in 1971 was: BMC 250JU, £2,793; Mercedes 408, £4,695. Another Cotswold model popular during the early 1970s was the Caravelle, based on the Ford Transit 130 chassis. Although more box-like in appearance than the larger Concorde, it was basically a smaller version of its bigger stablemate. Interior finishing was similar; so too was the three-quarter-berth option with bunk beds once again behind the cab area. The Caravelle was priced at £2,095 in 1972.

By far the largest option in the Cotswold range was the big Austin FG D-Series. In external appearance it was very rectangular with little body styling used to disguise its angular lines. The interior was of typical Cotswold finish – acres of storage space, a very well-equipped kitchen and that familiar wood-effect laminate finish to all surfaces. If you had to ask the price of a D-Series, it is very likely you couldn't afford one! Very few were built and I know of only one surviving example that is still in use within the UK.

Towards the end of Cotswold production in the mid-1970s, the company produced a wonderful one-off motorcaravan on the ill-fated A-Series Ford chassis. The A-Series Ford was released in 1973 and it was intended that this new model would compete with the Mercedes 408; it borrowed many interior fittings from the best-selling Transit. Cotswold printed a full-colour brochure for the new A-Series motorcaravan, but only one was ever built. Based on the A0510 chassis, it was 21ft (6,400mm) long and was powered by the V6 3ltr petrol engine. This particular Cotswold was given instant stardom when it was offered as a competition prize by the *Daily Express* newspaper. Contestants had to list, in order of importance, the various plus points of the vehicle, which was being displayed at Earls Court. The winner was a Miss Jocelyn Lukins from London. She was presented with the keys to the vehicle by radio and television personality Cliff Michelmore at the International Caravan and Camping Exhibition. Despite her initial delight at winning this Cotswold, she accepted a cash alternative and the vehicle was returned to Ford. The company used the motorcaravan as a publicity vehicle at many events throughout 1974 including Henley. But by January 1975, Ford had sold it to a former works engineer who happened to be a keen motorcaravanner. He and his wife used the vehicle until 1990, then until 1997 it sat on his drive, unused. My own brother-in-law purchased the Cotswold Commander with a view to restoring it to its former glory (water ingress had taken its toll on the interior by this time). Due to work commitments, however, he had to face the fact that he simply didn't have the time for a full restoration and it was sold to an enthusiast. The vehicle hasn't been seen since. This Cotswold Commander once held (and possibly still does?) a rather dubious record, the fastest motorcaravan to drive in reverse around the Brands Hatch racetrack!

ABOVE: *One of the most popular models in the Cotswold range was the C-Series, a coach-built model available on the BMC J2 and 250JU chassis. This was again a side entrance camper with rear dinette/bed. Pictured here on a club rally is a very good example based on the BMC 250JU.*

LEFT: *The interior of the C-Series Cotswold did differ very slightly, depending upon the base vehicle. This is the kitchen area within the C-Series on the BMC 250JU. The cooker has been placed directly behind the driver's cab, the result being that one had to leave the living area to access the cab and vice versa.*

TOP: An extremely rare sight discovered in Scotland several years ago, this is one of the early Cotswold high-top conversions on the BMC J2. Years ahead of its time, the public in the early 1960s just weren't ready for GRP high-top examples. I don't believe that it left the Cotswold factory with those frontal graphics!

ABOVE: Released by Cotswold in the early 1970s was the Caravelle, only available on the Ford Transit. Another side entrance model which, despite its compact appearance, was surprisingly spacious inside.

RIGHT: Certainly the flagship of the whole Cotswold range, this is the D-Series Cotswold based on the BMC FG chassis. It is believed that very few were produced, but one restored example is a regular around the classic shows and rally scene in the UK.

13

Debonair

Front view of the Debonair with the unmistakable grille and nose section of the Bedford CA. Note the raised roofline along the centre of the camper giving full standing height. Extra windows above the normal windscreen also made the cab area very light.

DEBONAIR – BEDFORD CA

Released by Martin Walter Ltd in 1964, the Dormobile Debonair certainly took centre stage for innovative design and styling. In fact, the Debonair couldn't easily be classified, as it wasn't a coach-built example in the traditional sense, but nor was it a panel van conversion. The craftsmen at the Folkestone factory broke new ground by constructing a motorcaravan using a one-piece, glass-fibre moulded model. Due to the very long association that the company had with Vauxhall Motors, the Debonair was only available based on the Bedford CA, 15/17cwt base. Only the small CA metal bonnet and grille section were retained; the remainder of the vehicle was a complete GRP moulding. The

Debonair, released in 1964, continued in production on the Bedford CA until the introduction of the new Bedford CF in 1969. It was then restyled for the new base vehicle. For the purpose of this model description, a model from 1966 is being detailed.

The Dormobile design team certainly brought all their years of experience to the fore when committing the Debonair to paper. This model had one of the most noticeable exteriors of any motorcaravan from the classic period. The front end was distinctively Bedford CA, although just above the windscreen two separate long windows were added for extra internal light. Two further deep quadrant windows were placed to either side of the windscreen, giving the driver excellent views of the road yet at

the same time allowing even more light into the motorcaravan interior. At the rear of the vehicle were more beautifully shaped windows letting the light come flooding into the rear section. The GRP body afforded full standing height within the interior and two opening roof ventilators were fitted as standard. The interior of this model was neatly divided into two sections, or cabins as Dormobile referred to them. The forward area contained the cooker, an Eas-icool food storage cabinet (or optional fridge) and forward-facing seats for five people. The rear cabin was fitted with lounge-type seating, which became the dinette when the table was erected.

Upon opening the one-piece rear door, one was confronted by the lounge/dinette. Textile-covered seating was to each interior side of the vehicle and a table (stored beneath a seat) could be erected with the aid of two metal legs and was placed between the seats for dining. The remainder of this cabin consisted of eye-level storage lockers, with further storage beneath the seat bases. The dinette seats converted at night into a double bed. All exterior surfaces within the dinette/lounge were finished in a wood veneer. Two good size wardrobes were also within this area of the vehicle, situated near the middle on each side. When viewed from the rear a tall cupboard could be seen on the left, next to a wardrobe. This housed the toilet and had a square louvre window mounted quite high within it. The forward cabin was a further seating area, containing forward-facing seats for five people (including the driver). These seats converted into a second double bed. Easy access to the frontal area could be gained (in addition to the rear) via the passenger cab door.

RIGHT: Dormobile Debonair, the all-GRP-bodied camper by Martin Walter Ltd (Dormobile). This cutaway drawing is self-explanatory, showing the various features of this rather unique model.
BELOW: The original press launch photograph of the Debonair, a new concept in motorcaravan design for the mid-1960s by one of the leading coachbuilders in the UK. The bonnet and nose cowl were all that remained of the Bedford CA base vehicle on the exterior. A multitude of windows made this model's interior very light and airy. Access was either via the single rear door or through the cab.

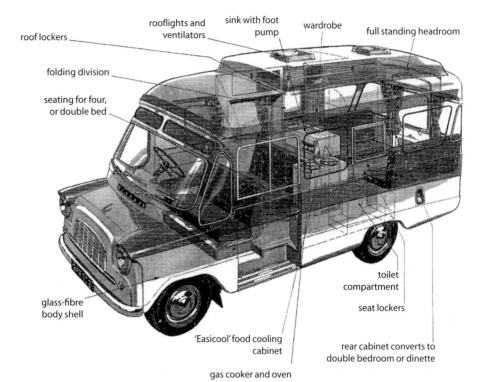

roof lockers — rooflights and ventilators — sink with foot pump — wardrobe — full standing headroom

folding division

seating for four, or double bed

glass-fibre body shell

'Easicool' food cooling cabinet

gas cooker and oven

toilet compartment

seat lockers

rear cabinet converts to double bedroom or dinette

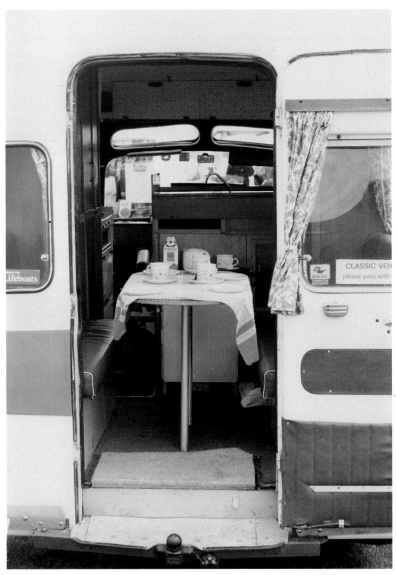

The kitchen in the Debonair was extremely well planned for such a confined space, with the possible exception of the fridge, as this was situated in a slightly awkward position opposite the cooker in a narrow gap. The stainless-steel sink was housed in the dividing cupboard, which separated the front and rear areas. Water was pumped to the sink via a foot-operated system; this in turn came from three 3gal (14ltr) containers. The containers were accessed via a floor well, the floor section being clipped to a bracket on the seat (a water heater was an optional extra). Gas bottles were also housed in the floor; again a floor section was removed for access and this was near the toilet/sink area. The cooker, with oven, was placed near the toilet and wardrobe, just behind the passenger seat. The cooker had a fold-up worktop and there was a high-mounted storage cupboard above. Surfaces within the forward area were finished in a bright, hard-wearing laminate. The Easicool storage cabinet (or optional fridge) was beneath the sink and accessed from the end.

A very clever folding door/flap system was employed on this model. The designers certainly hadn't missed a trick on the Debonair and even came up with a very simple way of dividing the front and rear cabins by means of both the toilet door and other flaps. These were bolted into fittings to provide the Debonair interior with two completely separate areas, ideal for privacy. During my research there was a recurring

Anyone for afternoon tea? This really nice example was on display at a motorcaravan show, in order to give the public a taste of motorcaravanning during the boom years of sales. The Debonair was a very well-designed model, a camper in two halves, with the kitchen facilities dividing the internal living space.

This side view of the Debonair gives a clear indication of just how many windows were fitted in this model. The triangular window in the cab gave excellent vision for the driver. At the far end of this picture is a very rare Ford Thames Hadrian, alongside a VW Danbury conversion.

Press release photograph of the interior, revealing a clever use of confined space by the Dormobile designers. Both front and rear sections contained a double bed. The central kitchen seen here divided them.

theme when reading about previous test reports of this model carried out over the years since its introduction. Everyone mentioned the enormous amount of storage space that Dormobile had managed to fit into this unique motorcaravan, given its dimensions. It was clearly designed by someone who had actually used a motorcaravan, which surprisingly was not always the case with some conversions!

Curtains were fitted as standard to all windows on this model and fluorescent lighting was fitted to both rear and forward areas. Martin Walter Ltd offers a bewildering array of options for all Dormobile models and the Debonair was no exception. Basic options for the Bedford CA base vehicle were a four-speed gearbox (in place of the standard three-speed); a diesel engine was an extra £125 in late 1966, early 1967. Specific to this model was the option of a fridge in place of the Easicool cabinet at £45, a water heater at £35 and concertina-style blinds for the windows above the cab at £3/5s. The price listing for a Dormobile Debonair early in 1967 was £1,298 in basic/standard form.

One very interesting feature to note in relation to this model concerned the exterior colour. Paint colours on the Debonair GRP body were bonded into

the shell during manufacture, a unique feature for this period. The standard Dormobile colours for the main body area were (in 1967): Dormobile White, Iris Blue, Foam Grey and Lime Green. The nose section, top coach line and vehicle side flash could be painted in any Martin Walter colour, of which there were many. As a point of reference, by far the most common colour combination for the Debonair was to have the main body in Dormobile White with the coach lines in a burgundy/red. The sales brochure of the period stated 'repainting could be forgotten – the colour, bonded into the material during manufacture, keeps its lustre'. I don't expect that Martin Walter

Ltd thought for a moment that Debonair models would still be in use forty years later! Fading of the colours has now occurred on many surviving examples due to weathering and repainting has had to be undertaken. The Bedford CA Dormobile Debonair was a great success story for the Folkestone company. It was hugely popular from the outset in 1964, received excellent press reviews and indeed remains a very sought-after classic motorcaravan today.

When the Bedford CA finally ceased production and was replaced by the CF model in 1969, the Debonair name was carried over to the new model in the form of the Dormobile Debonair II.

Brochure cover picture.

14

ERF Roadranger

ABOVE: Not exactly a standard paint colour, but stunning all the same. The ERF Roadranger was a side entry model, with drop-down access step. The vents visible on the side of the bodywork denote the placement of the fridge within the interior. Also evident here is the standard Transit front grille, with a flat appearance. This implies that the 2ltr petrol engine was fitted. This particular example was given the name 'Gremlin' by its owners, who won many awards with it during the 1990s. It has sadly disappeared from the classic camper scene in recent years.

The author's 1974 Ford Transit ERF Roadranger. This model was produced for around three years, ceasing production in 1975. Just over 200 were built by Jennings, the body division of ERF Ltd. Both the interior and exterior styling were completely different to the earlier Jennings Roadrangers. This Transit has the bull-nose front end, as the original engine was the 2.5ltr petrol unit, later upgraded to the 3ltr Essex engine. It has now been fitted with a more economical 2.5ltr diesel engine from a much later Transit.

ERF ROADRANGER – FORD TRANSIT

When the ERF Roadranger was unveiled in 1973 it met with a very mixed reception, no doubt largely due to the strange exterior styling of the over-cab frontal area. Whereas the rear coach-built section followed the standard design elements of the time, the integral roof and frontal GRP moulding was certainly a break with tradition. Whatever one's thoughts on exterior styling, internally this was a coach-build of the highest specifications and indeed was one of the most expensive UK models of the time. I have to admit to being the owner of a 1974 example, but will aim to be as objective as I can with my analysis of the Roadranger!

This model was based on the Ford Transit 130 chassis; standard power came from a 2ltr V4 petrol unit but a 2.5ltr V6 petrol, with an overdrive gearbox, was an optional extra. In press literature, the company stated that the ERF Roadranger was also available on the Bedford CF. Only one model is thought to remain based on the Bedford and this could possibly have been the very model produced by the company as a prototype for road tests by various publications. A total of 205 ERF Road-rangers were built between 1973–75 and at least one was constructed using the A-Series Ford chassis. All these models were built by ERF Ltd, Body Division at Sandbach, Cheshire.

This model was hand-built using tra-ditional coachbuilding methods – an aluminium skin was fixed to a hardwood frame. The roof and front moulding were all one-piece GRP and the vehicle was insulated throughout with glass-fibre wool. It featured large sliding win-dows to each side and access to the interior was via a side entrance door on the nearside rear. In standard form this was a luxury two-berth model, but two children could be accommodated in the area above the cab with a safety rail and access ladder ordered as an extra. There was also the option of having a stretcher bunk in the cab area. When ordering this model from new, buyers were also able to request two single beds in place of the standard double.

Turning to the interior description, access to the living area was via a one-piece door to the rear nearside, with a fold-down step situated at the base of this door. Upon entering the Roadranger there was a toilet/shower cubicle imme-diately ahead, located in the offside cor-ner. This consisted of a showerhead with mixer taps, chemical toilet and fold-down washbasin. A 12V light was fixed to the ceiling and a frosted glass window allowed light in during the day. The door of this cubicle had a further door attached to the inside. These two doors would then swing around and clip to the rear wall of the interior, thus giving the user much more space and, of course, pri-vacy. Alongside the toilet/shower cubi-cle were the main kitchen units. There was a full cooker with oven and grill at one end; next to this was the stainless-steel sink and drainer. Cupboards below the sink featured a twin-door cabinet and a chest of drawers. The cooker was also hidden when not in use by means of matching cabinet doors. A split worktop concealed both the sink and cooker; this was of a light wood laminate with black laminate edging. The worktop over the cooker hinged back against the interior wall of the vehicle, whereas the worktop covering the sink/drainer not only hinged back, but would also slide along,

Rear view of the ERF Roadranger, showing the large rear window with a frosted section in the shower/toilet compartment. The coach-built body consisted of the traditional aluminium panels over a hardwood frame. The rear spare wheel carrier and bike rack holder are non-standard fittings.

The rather bulbous over-cab styling was not everyone's cup of tea when introduced; it was certainly different and some thought it rather hideous. The long oval window above was an optional extra, as it made the over-cab area slightly brighter if used as a child's bed. On the two-berth model this area would have been for storage only.

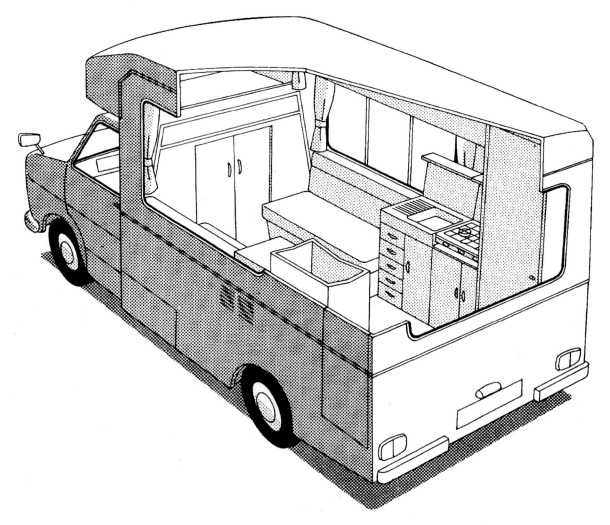

OPPOSITE PAGE:

TOP: *The reason why Ford fitted two different style fronts to the MK I Transit cab – the 2.5ltr and 3ltr engines simply would not fit into the conventional engine bay. The rather curved bull-nose version offered several more vital inches to the front. This particular engine is the 3ltr V6 Essex.*

BOTTOM: *This cutaway drawing shows the interior features of the ERF Roadranger quite clearly. Immediately opposite the rear-side entrance door was the full-height shower/toilet compartment. To the left of this was the stainless-steel sink/drainer and full cooker. Storage cupboards and drawers were below these fixtures. Opposite the kitchen was a full-size wardrobe with hanging rail and shelving. To the side of this was the large-capacity gas/electric fridge, with worktop above. Dinette/seating area were just behind the driving cab, although the dividing doors illustrated were in fact optional extras. Dining table was stored in a clever locker just above the cab dividing doors in the picture. Cold-water storage tank was located under the dinette seat, with the waste tank attached to the rear chassis.*

THIS PAGE:

ERF Roadranger interior with dining table in position; this stored away in the locker seen here above the occupants. Other features evident in this picture are the larger fridge just to the left, storage lockers running along each side at head height and the blanked-off panel in the over-cab area (optional window).

thus creating extra working space. Mixer taps were situated directly behind the sink, drawing water from the freshwater tank located below the dinette seat.

Moving back to the entrance door once again, from this position there was a full-height wardrobe to the left with hanging rail and upper shelf. This wardrobe also had an automatic light fitted, which came on when the door was opened. The base of the wardrobe housed the rear of the gas fire and associated fittings. Turning left into the living area one was faced with the side of the wardrobe to the left, on the base of which was fixed the gas fire. At eye level was a large mirror. Situated next to the wardrobe (and opposite the kitchen) was the large-capacity fridge. This was housed within a unit and had a worktop above, finished once again in light wood-effect laminate. A small wooden hatch below the fridge gave access to the gas tap for isolating purposes. Also in this area was located a mains power point and two 12V outlets for accessories. The remainder of the interior space was allocated to the dinette and seating area. This was directly behind the main vehicle cab and consisted of two inward-facing bench-style seats, which were finished in textile upholstery. The table for dining was located in a clever housing within the base of the over-cab storage area. A wooden panel pulled down to reveal the table, which could then slide out, clipping into holders at the back of the cab. The table was finished in the same light wood laminate as the worktops; a metal leg attached to the table base unclipped for support.

Next to the housing for the table storage was another, smaller pull-down wooden flap, and this contained the wooden slats that were required for making up the bed. Beneath the seat bases were large storage areas, with the

exception of one, which, as previously stated, was home to the freshwater tank and electric water pump. Both the seats on each side and the back supports were incorporated into the double bed. If a children's bunk was not specified in the over-cab area, then this of course became another enormous area for storage. In addition to the storage found in the kitchen area and below the seat bases, there were eye-level cupboards running along each side of the interior. These hinged upwards with self-locking stays to keep the doors open.

As noted above, the Roadranger had two large sliding windows at each side, but it also had a large rear window and

a bus-style roof vent to the centre of the vehicle, making it an extremely light and airy interior. Fluorescent lighting was fitted to the interior as standard; this consisted of ceiling lights at each end of the vehicle and a light on the base of an eye-level cupboard over the kitchen. A high-quality carpet was fitted to the main floor of the living area with vinyl cushion flooring fitted to the entrance area near the rear door.

The interior furniture within this model was constructed from sapele-veneered blockboard, although an oak veneer finish could be ordered in lieu of the standard sapele. Another feature ordered by many ERF Roadranger

LEFT: This is the interior of the prototype, which is slightly confusing as the cooker and sink/drainer actually swapped sides when the ERF Roadranger went into full-time production. The worktops seen here in the raised position were on a sliding mechanism, the longer section being capable of being positioned way over the seating to that side.

buyers was the optional double sliding doors behind the driving compartment, which screened the driving cab from the living area and afforded complete privacy. Curtains were fitted to all windows within the living area as standard, together with Venetian blinds. When it came to the list of optional extras on offer for this model, they were quite extensive and included single-bed extensions, stretcher bunk in cab, oak veneer finish, mains-operated air-conditioning unit, fly screens, extractor fan, rear stabilizing jacks, complete vehicle undersealing and chrome rear quarter bumpers in place of the standard painted items.

As previously mentioned, this model was at the high end of the price scale during its limited production span – the cost of an ERF Roadranger (in standard form) during the spring of 1974 would have been around £4,000. During my many years of motorcaravan ownership it was the vehicle that I always aspired to. When I did finally get the opportunity to purchase one from a friend I certainly wasn't disappointed, as it has been everything I expected it to be. However, despite its luxury classic appeal, this model is not without its minor faults. Firstly, the fuel filler is extremely difficult to access through the ERF coachwork, and secondly the upper roof moulding was poorly designed. For some reason, the designers decided to put a deep inverted cavity into the top roof section on the vehicle, most likely in order to aid the build process. In effect, though, it creates a small swimming pool on the roof after any rainfall. The consequence of this is that one gets an unwelcome shower when opening the rear entrance door after it has been raining!

Roadranger II
based on the new Ford 'A' series chassis/cab

LEFT: Artist's impression of the ERF Roadranger based on the A-Series Ford; knowledgeable Roadranger enthusiasts are, however, quite confident that only one example was ever produced.

15

Freeway

Bedford CF Dormobile Freeway. This artist's drawing dates from 1974 and the cutaway feature gives an excellent view of the Freeway's interior.

FREEWAY – DORMOBILE BEDFORD CF AND FORD TRANSIT

The issue of Martin Walter Ltd and the name Dormobile can appear somewhat confusing to many. In fact, the matter is quite straightforward – Martin Walter Ltd of Folkestone devised the term/name Dormobile to describe its utility vehicles during the 1950s and the name later became synonymous with motorcaravans throughout the UK. This began to happen to such an extent that a motorcaravan in general would be referred to, quite wrongly, as a Dormobile. A Dormobile motorcaravan was actually only genuine if produced by the Martin Walter factory; it was a brand name. However, as with all major companies that trade over a large number of years there are inevitable changes in both

management and structure. Such was the case with Martin Walter Ltd. The Dormobile brand name eventually became Dormobile Limited and was then a member of the giant Charringtons Group. The new company emblem, a blue letter D, was designed to represent the famous Dormobile side-lifting roof.

The company switched its best-selling model names, Romany and Debonair, from the Bedford CA to the Bedford CF in 1969, to coincide with the release of the new CF range of light commercials. Both models evolved fairly quickly, the Debonair becoming the Landcruiser and the Romany becoming the Freeway. This chapter will focus upon the highly successful panel van conversion with the famous Dormobile rising roof, the Dormobile Freeway. The second section of the chapter will focus on the

Freeway model from 1973 based on the Ford Transit 90 van, but we will start with a look at the Freeway based on the Bedford CF 22cwt van from 1974.

The CF-based Freeway was a conversion of the 22cwt van; a petrol engine was fitted as standard with a diesel option available. This was a panel van conversion, so naturally the side-hinged Dormobile roof was employed. Fitted slightly forward of the GRP roof capping was a contoured roof rack, again moulded in GRP. Entrance into the Freeway was via twin opening rear doors. Inside, one was confronted with a traditional panel van layout with furniture positioned along each interior wall and the lounge/dinette just behind the driving compartment. These dinette seats (facing inwards for dining) could be altered to face forwards, thus giving four forward-

ABOVE: *Many of the surviving Dormobile Freeway models will by now have been repainted at some stage. This early model has been treated to a bright red colour scheme, with matching replacement fabric to the rising roof.*

LEFT: *Period press picture taken in 1973 of the Freeway interior. In this shot the table is in position between the inward-facing seats. These seats could also be arranged into two forward-facing seats for travelling.*

facing seats for travelling (although once again in line with most panel van conversions of this period, no rear seat belts were fitted). The clever Dormobile seating configuration allowed for the two front seats, together with the rear ones, to become two single beds as an option to the double converted from the dinette. The spacious rising roof housed two stretcher bunks, both measuring 6 feet in length. A further option for accommodating another child for sleeping was in a stretcher bunk within the driving compartment.

Viewing the interior from the rear doors, there was a kitchen to the right-hand side. This consisted of a two-burner hob and grill, sink unit with water pumped from a 12gal (55ltr) underfloor tank and various storage lockers and cupboards. The units were finished in a wood-grain melamine. Split worktops on top of the sink and cooker hinged upwards to act as splashbacks. Opposite the kitchen was a wardrobe unit and situated next to this was either a dresser unit, or the optional fridge (placed above both of these options was a large vanity mirror). Two further storage pockets were built onto the interior of the rear doors. Seating within the Freeway was finished in a nylon and tweed fabric, while the floor covering was carpet laid over a Vynolay base. Even the cab area did not escape the Dormobile design touch, the dash being finished in a rose-wood laminate. Curtains to all windows and fluorescent lighting complemented the remaining interior.

The Freeway was available in a huge array of body colour options from the Dormobile range. There were a couple of special edition Freeway models released during production, one being the Pink Freeway with a bright pink body colour, but if any now survive they have probably been repainted at some stage in a more conventional colour! Another special Freeway was the Tan Top model. On this model the GRP roof capping had a tan colour impregnated into it during manufacture (including the front roof rack). Also on this model, the traditional red and white candy stripes on the roof fabric were changed to tan, brown and white stripes. Dormobile also offered a variation on the CF Freeway around this time entitled the Calypso. The roof was enlarged slightly on this model and the tan, brown and white roof fabric was

RIGHT: Interior diagrams of the seating/sleeping plan. The top diagram shows seats arranged for either travel or dining. Middle diagram illustrates that two single beds can be formed, utilizing the seats in the driving cab. Bottom picture is the Freeway interior at night, with dinette seats converted to a double bed and single bed within the driving cab.

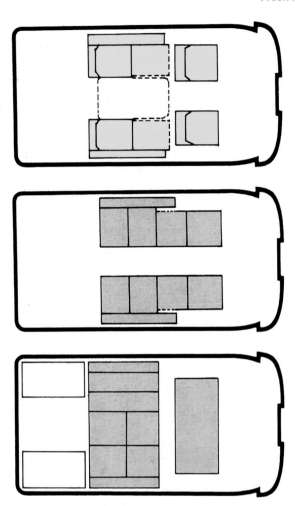

BELOW: There were a couple of limited-edition Freeway models produced by Dormobile; this is the Tan Top model. It was aimed at the person who wanted to use their Freeway as an everyday car-cum-office, not unlike the people carriers of today. The GRP roof capping on this model was tan, and the rising roof fabric was tan and brown stripes.

New tan top Freeway

The roof, of course, is Dormobile's unique creation, and with the latest model — the Tan Top Freeway — this sleek roof design gets an exciting new touch of colour which transforms the Dormobile into a smart man-about-town vehicle when not in its holiday role.

BELOW: Sales brochure covers did vary each year throughout the production run of a particular model. Seen here is the cover of the brochure dating from 1973 with the Freeway parked on a beach.

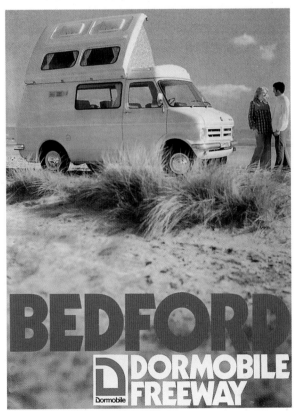

Freeway

RIGHT: *The very popular Freeway model was not confined solely to the Bedford CF Chassis. Buyers also had the option of the Ford Transit as a base vehicle, seen here as an artist's cutaway drawing.*

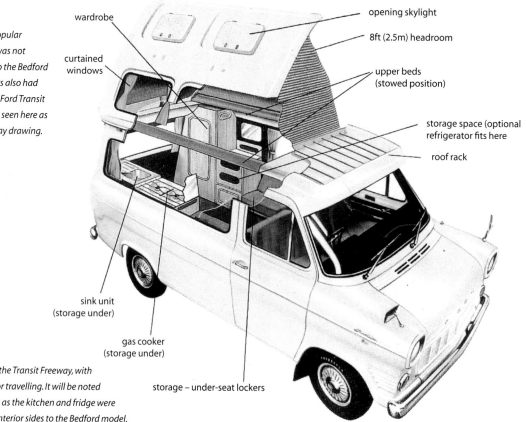

wardrobe

opening skylight

curtained windows

8ft (2.5m) headroom

upper beds (stowed position)

storage space (optional refrigerator fits here

roof rack

sink unit (storage under)

gas cooker (storage under)

storage – under-seat lockers

BELOW: *Interior of the Transit Freeway, with seats arranged for travelling. It will be noted that fixtures such as the kitchen and fridge were on the opposite interior sides to the Bedford model.*

retained from the Tan Top special. The interior was also revamped, with the kitchen and fridge switching sides within the interior. Other changes included a darker laminate finish to all surfaces and a very distinctive flash decal to each side of the exterior. One of the most distinctive features of the Calypso was the tinted windows, designed to give the occupants more privacy.

The cost of a Dormobile Freeway based on the Bedford CF in 1974 would have been in the order of £2,500.

Whereas the Freeway based on the Bedford CF had been a development of the earlier CF Romany, the Freeway based on the Ford Transit had evolved from the earlier Dormobile Transit models, the Enterprise and Explorer. Both had been panel van conversions with a

rising roof based upon the popular Transit van. The Ford Transit Freeway was based on the Transit 90 chassis with the 1.7ltr petrol engine; a diesel option was not offered although automatic transmission was. The same roofline design principle was used on the Ford offering as had been seen on the CF Freeway. The side-hinged rising roof with a roof rack was incorporated into the front to form a very nice streamlined appearance. The red and white candy stripes on the roof fabric were evident here once again. Another similarity between the CF option and the Transit was the light Melamine finish to all interior cupboards. The seating, dinette and sleeping configurations were also exactly the same on the Transit model. The only major deviation came with the rear cupboard placement and on the Transit the kitchen was moved to the right-hand side when viewed from the rear door. The wardrobe, vanity mirror and dresser/fridge were opposite. One other feature of note was that the majority of Transit Freeway models were based on the chassis with the one-piece rear-lifting tailgate, as opposed to twin opening doors. The body colour was limited on the Transit to just White, Red or Primrose. The cost of a Dormobile Freeway on the Transit base *circa* 1973 would have been around £2,500.

16

Hadrian

The Hadrian by Motor Caravan Bodies Ltd was the first coach-built example to be built upon the new Commer chassis when it was released in 1960. The Hadrian Commanche was a well-styled model with side entrance access door.

HADRIAN – COMMER

Motor Caravan Bodies Ltd of Newburn, Newcastle-upon-Tyne, built the Hadrian range of coach-built motorcaravans. This coachbuilding company was at one time a specialist boat builder, later progressing to the increasingly popular motorcaravan industry. The name chosen for the range of models to be offered was taken from the famous Roman wall in the north of England. The company only produced motorcaravans for around four to five years, always coach-built models. However, it does hold one claim to fame within the history and development of leisure vehicles, as it was the first company to offer a coach-built model for sale on the new release from Rootes in 1960, the Commer.

The Hadrian range included four models: the Ambassador on the Ford Thames 15cwt chassis; the Austral based on the Austin 152; the Bedouin on the Bedford CA; and finally the Commanche on the Commer 15cwt. Judging by press articles and period publications, it appears that the most popular model was that based on the Commer, the Hadrian Commanche. This chapter will therefore concentrate on this model for description purposes, although the interior of each model was pretty much of a standard design. The son of one of the original company owners revealed that the design for the Hadrian was in fact based upon a trailer caravan that the family had used to tour Ireland. The company certainly did manage to capture the caravan feel

with the Hadrian design; even its external appearance owed much to the early touring caravans of a bygone era.

The Hadrian was rather box-like in appearance, with a contoured roof of three sections constructed from GRP. The rear section was perhaps the most elaborate design feature of the exterior, with a curved waistline and nice aluminium beading to emphasize the detailing. The rear windows were in three sections, with one-piece windows at each end with a square louvre window in the centre. The access flap for the water tank was also on the rear end. Entry to the living area of the Hadrian was via a side entrance door positioned just behind the passenger cab door. A fold-down step nicely recessed into the bottom of the door

ABOVE: The factory workforce stand proudly beside a Hadrian. This picture, taken in the early 1960s, features a Hadrian based upon the Bedford CA.

LEFT: Rear view of the Commer Hadrian. This section was contoured around the waistline with detailed aluminium trim. The rear had two fixed windows to either side and louvre windows to the centre. The small square access hatch seen to the left of the right-hand rear lens was the water-filler aperture.

aided access into the vehicle. The top half of the entrance door was glazed and again the designers had used aluminium beading to the exterior of the door, which continued in a coach line/flash along the side of the Hadrian, just below the window line.

The kitchen facilities were located along the rear of the vehicle and included a sink, cooker with oven and spacious storage units. Water was delivered to the sink via a hand pump, located to one side of the sink. A cool cabinet was fitted as standard, although a fridge could be ordered as an option. In the nearside rear corner was an extremely large wardrobe, so big in fact that this was often used as a toilet compartment. Eye-level storage lockers were in abundance all around the interior and the space above the driving cab was more than large enough for all bedding and pillows. The table in the Hadrian was of the free-standing variety and dining took place in a central area of the vehicle. The Hadrian had four forward-facing seats (including those in the driving cab) and a longer bench-style seat towards the rear, near the kitchen. This seat converted into a double bed, as did the seats within the central part of the vehicle, making this a four-berth model. If a two-berth model was specified, then the single seat directly behind the driver's seat was replaced with a narrow wardrobe.

Interior of the Commer Hadrian, looking towards the rear. This model had the kitchen area fitted along the rear interior of the vehicle. The tall cupboard to the right rear corner was the combined wardrobe/toilet.

View from the rear kitchen of the front area. For travelling, four people could face forwards and three could be seated on the rear bench seat. Mirror fronts can be seen here to the storage area above the driving cab. There were additional storage lockers all around the interior at head height.

The interior of the Hadrian was panelled in a light oak veneer; cupboard and door edges were also made from oak with oak veneer again being used for the door inserts on cupboards. Fresh water was carried in a 10gal (46ltr) underfloor tank; a waste tank was also fitted to the vehicle's underside. All seating was covered with a textile upholstery fabric in several colour options. The standard floor covering was vinyl but a carpet was available as an option; curtains were fitted to all windows as standard. Lighting within the living area was supplied from both gas and electric fitments.

The Hadrian range certainly consisted of well-constructed models with a good interior design. Despite the fact that they were available for about five years, very few examples survive.

Although the Commer Commanche four-berth model was described above, given here are the prices for all models in the 1964 line-up: the Hadrian Ambassador (Ford Thames) £1,060; Hadrian Austral (Austin 152) £1,090; Hadrian Bedouin (Bedford CA) £1,083; and the Hadrian Commanche on the Commer, £1,083.

LEFT: *Another view of the kitchen facilities, with the hand-operated water pump evident to the rear of the worktop. The sink was to the left and cooker to the right. On this model some cupboard space has been sacrificed in order to fit a fridge.*

ABOVE: *The Hadrian body was available on the Austin 152, Bedford CA, Commer and Ford Thames. This is a 1964 Ford Thames example. There are only two known Thames Hadrian models in the UK.*
LEFT: *The same Thames Hadrian, this time seen from the rear. The facilities lockers on the rear have been clearly marked on this example, gas and water. This particular Hadrian has been laid up for some years, but is now thankfully being restored.*

17

Highwayman

ABOVE: Early press picture of the Commer Highwayman by Bluebird. The Highwayman coach-build was first released in 1958 based on the BMC J2. Once mated to the Commer chassis it became the best-selling coach-built model of the 1960s.

BELOW: Although the basic exterior shape remained pretty much the same throughout production on the Commer, some minor changes were made. By the 1970s the aluminium exterior detail trim to the sides had given way to a more modern finish. This nicely preserved example is seen here on display at a motorcaravan show in the early 1990s; this model is still in use today.

HIGHWAYMAN – COMMER

Bluebird Caravans Ltd first released the Highwayman model back in 1958. It was only available on the BMC J2 chassis at that time. It would continue in production for over twenty years, but it would be the 1960s and early 1970s when it was achieving most success with high sales figures. When Rootes released the Commer in 1960 it wasn't long before the Highwayman was transferred from the BMC base over to the Commer chassis. Already a relative success on the BMC J2, its popularity increased beyond all expectations when it was coupled with the Commer. In fact, such was the success of the Commer Highwayman by 1964 that

Commer Cars agreed to drop its own conversion on the panel van, the Commer Maidstone, in order to concentrate all of its efforts into supplying base vehicles for the Highwayman body. It proved to be good business sense, as the Commer Highwayman became the biggest selling coach-built motorcaravan of the 1960s.

The exterior shape of the Highwayman changed little over the years – there were detailed modifications to some body sections but a Highwayman is a pretty unmistakable model, whether it is from the early 1960s or mid-'70s. As the mid-1960s were the very peak of the Highwayman success story, this chapter will concentrate on the 1966 model. Firstly, it would be a little unfair to describe the Highwayman as 'cheap and cheerful', but as far as craftsmanship was concerned, it simply wasn't in the same league as some coach-built models like the Paralanian or Jennings Roadranger. This was a no-nonsense, no-frills coach-build that was designed to appeal to families, which was evident by the fact that even in standard form the Highwayman would sleep five people, six with the optional stretcher bunk. Despite having a total length of only 15ft 4in (4,674mm), the designers had worked miracles with the interior proportions of this model, giving the impression that it was in fact far bigger than those dimensions suggested.

The 1966 model had the distinctive box-like appearance associated with the Highwayman throughout production, with aluminium and GRP panels clad over a hardwood timber frame. The roof with its domed shape to the over-cab area was made up of four separate sections with a large translucent roof panel, which lifted up for ventilation purposes. The Highwayman was a rear-entry model featuring a single door with glazed top panel; a fold-down step was provided to assist with access to the interior. Standing at the rear of the interior one was presented with an enormous seating area, which ran the whole length of the right-hand side. These well-upholstered seats were fitted with moquette covers. These seats were divided into two sections, the first, longer seat finishing just short of the forward dinette area. This long seat converted into a double bed when

the base was pulled out and the back cushions laid flat.

Opposite this long seat was a wardrobe/toilet compartment in the left-hand corner, followed by the kitchen units. The kitchen consisted of a sink with drainer, storage cupboards beneath and a cooker with an oven on the end. If the optional fridge was specified, the buyer had to sacrifice the oven, as the fridge was then fitted below a two-burner hob with grill. Some customers had a fridge fitted

after purchase and preferred to sacrifice one of the kitchen base cupboards, rather than the oven. Both the sink and cooker were fitted with worktops, which lifted back to act as splashbacks. Water was pumped to the sink via a foot-operated pump, which drew water from an underfloor tank. Further eye-level storage lockers were situated above the kitchen area and a gaslight was fixed to the side of the wardrobe, to supply light over the kitchen. The eye-level lockers over the kitchen were

Interior of 'BYM 512H' laid out for afternoon tea. The dinette seats seen here would form one double bed and the long settee near the entrance door (not pictured) would form another.

Production of the Highwayman based on the Commer came to an end in 1975, which makes this example one of the last. Earlier models had the rear lights set into a GRP-moulded corner panel; this was changed on later models with larger lights integrated into the flat aluminium rear panel.

mirrored on the opposite side, above the long seating, giving the Highwayman huge amounts of storage space.

The forward area of both the seating and kitchen, on the vehicle sides, was the dinette with free-standing table. This was the traditional configuration of two facing bench seats, which would convert into a double bed – therefore supplying two separate double beds within the living area. On both sides of the vehicle were very large windows with opening sections and curtains were supplied as standard for all windows. The area above the driving cab was an open hatch designed to be used for storage. Running in line with the cab roof at chest height was a roll-up stretcher bunk, which clipped into holders and hung over the dinette/double bed below. The interior was finished with a vinyl covering to the floor and all cupboards were finished with a wood-grain laminate. Gas bottles were housed in a compartment below the dinette seat and electric ceiling lights were fitted as standard (in addition to the single gaslight). As an optional

extra, a single stretcher bunk could be ordered (for a child) to fit across the driving cab.

Ownership of the Highwayman model has always been somewhat confusing. It was originally built by Bluebird Caravans Ltd and was therefore initially marketed as the Bluebird Highwayman. During the 1960s, the trailer caravan manufacturer Caravans International merged with Bluebird and this model then became the Highwayman by Caravans International (Motorized) Ltd, or CI/M for short. On 1 September 1973 the company name changed yet again, so for the final couple of years the Commer Highwayman was built by CI Autohomes Ltd. Throughout these changes in company name, the Highwayman was always built at factory premises in Poole, Dorset.

The Commer Highwayman model was one of the first UK-built motorcaravans to be sold successfully abroad. The man behind the overall success of the Highwayman model was Peter Duff, who decided to exhibit the Highwayman at the Californian Sportsman's

Show in 1965. It proved to be a huge success and orders for £2,800,000 worth of models were taken. For some reason, though, the names of the base vehicle and the model were changed for the USA market – gone was Commer Highwayman, and in came Sunbeam Funwagon. Although the vast majority of these models were shipped from Southampton, rather surprisingly eight couples flew over from the States to collect their vehicles from the factory. They then set off on a 20,000-mile journey through several countries and eventually back home! I'm pleased to say that nearly forty years later some of those Sunbeam Funwagons have survived the test of time and are still in use both in America and Canada.

The Commer Highwayman ceased production in 1975, although it was not to be the end for the model name. A completely new coach-built body was designed and mated to the new Leyland Sherpa chassis, and so began another successful chapter for a famous old model name.

One minor exterior change during production was the shape of the front over-cab moulding. On this early 1960s model it has a rather angular appearance, on later models it was far more rounded. Note on this example the standard wood-grain panel below the side window; this is an area of design detailing on the exterior that did change from time to time.

Interior view of the Commer Highwayman, looking towards the rear of the vehicle. Kitchen facilities were on the right with overhead lockers above. The toilet and wardrobe were in each rear corner. The long settee seen here was pulled out to form another double bed (in addition to the dinette).

When the Leyland Sherpa was released in 1975, the Highwayman body was completely redesigned and mated to the new base vehicle. This press picture demonstrates very clearly that the new Highwayman was different in every aspect to the earlier Commer version, although it remained a rear entry example.

Interior of the 'all-new' Leyland Highwayman. This picture shows the seating area arranged for dining purposes. The area above the driving cab on this model was a double bed, visible above the access door to the cab.

As the Commer Highwayman was in production for so many years, various retail prices will be given here for reference. A year after production began the original Highwayman based on the BMC J2 was £875; by 1964, and now based on the Commer, the cost was £950. In 1967 the price had increased beyond the £1,000 barrier to £1,100. During the final year of production the Highwayman carried a price tag of £2,500, by which time VAT had been introduced in the UK.

18

Holdsworth

ABOVE: The Leyland Sherpa with conversion by Richard Holdsworth Conversions Ltd. The Sherpa proved to be a popular choice for conversion from van to camper by many of the leading converters when it was introduced in 1975.

LEFT: Interior view of the Holdsworth Sherpa, looking back from the cab. The only problem that faced converters when tackling the Sherpa was the lack of width. This meant that no transverse bed was possible; instead designers had to work around a two single bed set-up. The inward-facing dinette seats seen here could be positioned as two forward-facing seats for travelling if preferred.

HOLDSWORTH – LEYLAND SHERPA

Richard Holdsworth began his conversion business in 1968. Richard had been working in Australia for eight years prior to returning to the UK. He and his wife, Heather, decided that they wanted a VW camper with which to explore the UK and the continent, but prices of new campers were prohibitive. They bought and converted a used VW Kombi van, and perfected the interior over thousands of miles of travelling. People were impressed with the conversion and Richard and Heather were frequently asked to build campers for others. Thus, in 1968, eighteen VW campers were converted inside a lock-up garage on Clapham Common, Richard building the furniture and Heather carrying out the trimming and upholstery.

A company offering VW spares asked Richard to build furniture kits for its customers, in order that they could fit out their own VW vans. From that moment, the manufacture and selling of Holdsworth furniture kits became an integral part of Richard Holdsworth Conversions. At this time, the VW spares company also offered Richard part of its factory at Ashford, Middlesex, as the lock-up garage had by that time become far too small. Business increased so much that just a year later they vacated the Ashford premises and moved to their third location in three years. This time, the business was moved to premises in Woodley, Berkshire, an ex-aerodrome hanger being the new factory location in 1972.

By the early 1970s Richard was offering six of his Holdsworth conversions. They consisted of a VW van conversion

The interior of the Holdsworth Sherpa with the two single beds made up. With this bed set-up there was plenty of clear floor space. Note the recess in the floor for an island-leg table.

This artist's drawing of the Sherpa gives an excellent insight into the Holdsworth conversion.

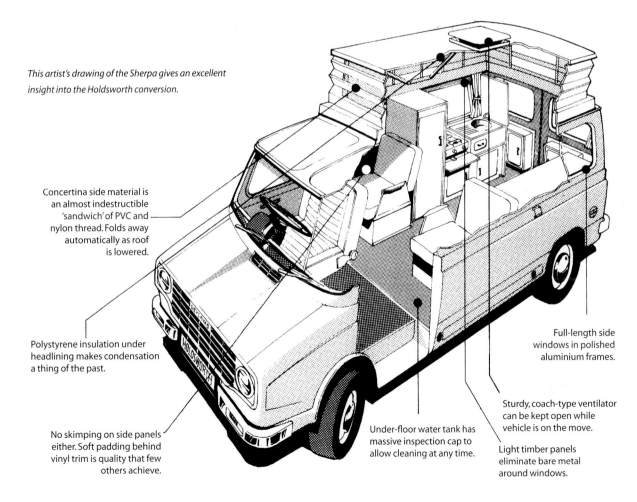

Concertina side material is an almost indestructible 'sandwich' of PVC and nylon thread. Folds away automatically as roof is lowered.

Polystyrene insulation under headlining makes condensation a thing of the past.

No skimping on side panels either. Soft padding behind vinyl trim is quality that few others achieve.

Under-floor water tank has massive inspection cap to allow cleaning at any time.

Full-length side windows in polished aluminium frames.

Sturdy, coach-type ventilator can be kept open while vehicle is on the move.

Light timber panels eliminate bare metal around windows.

with fixed roof, a Commer Standard, Commer Super, Bedford CF, Ford Transit and another VW, but this time with a rising roof. All of the conversions that were offered with a rising roof were fitted with the Weathershield vertically extending roof, the plastic sides of which unfolded in a concertina style when raised. This roof was in fact an improved version of the same roof as fitted to the Commer Maidstone from 1960. At the Holdsworth factory it was also possible to have a rising roof fitted to your non-Holdsworth motorcaravan or basic van ready for a self-fitting kit.

The line-up of Richard Holdsworth models remained pretty much unchanged until 1977 (with the exception of some varied layouts on the VW) when the Leyland Sherpa was added to his listing. The hierarchy at British Leyland were so impressed with the Sherpa Holdsworth that they gave their full company approval to the conversions. This was a panel van conversion of the popular Leyland Sherpa 230 Deluxe van, fitted with the 1.7ltr petrol engine; a 1.8ltr diesel was available, as was an automatic transmission option. This was a conversion of very good quality, with great attention to detail with regard to the placing of furniture within the interior.

The wardrobe, for example, was positioned on the driver's side, just behind the forward-facing rear seat, in order to avoid the blind spot on the rear nearside when driving.

With the exception of the wardrobe position, however, this was the traditional panel van layout. The twin rear doors had storage lockers built on to them. Looking forwards, towards the cab there was the kitchen to the right, with a stainless-steel sink nearest the rear door. A cooker was positioned next to the sink; this had a two-burner hob with grill. On top of the sink and cooker were the usual split worktops – the one over the cooker lifted up and back, the one over the sink lifted sideways towards the vehicle rear. The cupboard below these kitchen fixtures included a drawer, storage cupboard, lift-out rack for crockery and space for the gas bottle. This whole kitchen unit was located alongside the centrally located wardrobe. On the opposite side to the kitchen was a long storage cupboard incorporating three drawers. At the end of this cupboard was a food storage area, but an optional fridge could be fixed here at the buyer's request. This long storage unit was finished with a useful unobstructed worktop.

The dinette on this Holdsworth Sherpa was located in the traditional position, just behind the cab seats. But the dinette seats were not the normal bench type, which converted into the double bed. These were patented aircraft-style seats with armrests and quickly converted from dinette, inward-facing seats to two forward-facing seats. The seating was actually Dunlopillo foam covered in a rayon fabric, the cushion covers being fitted with zips for ease of cleaning. The table on this conversion used the 'new' principle of being supported by an island leg, thus doing away with legs at either end that often made access to the seats difficult. This means of supporting the table within a motorcaravan is of course now the accepted method used on all new models today.

Having already mentioned the dinette area, I didn't of course add that the dinette converted into the usual double bed, simply because it didn't. The Leyland Sherpa was of limited width (only 5ft 8in/1,727mm), so the dinette seat on either side, together with the cab seat, became single beds. This was a system employed on most panel van conversions based on the Sherpa. A kit was available as an option that enabled the owner to turn the two single beds

Holdsworth not only produced panel van conversions of the Leyland Sherpa, it also built an excellent coach-built example, the Holdsworth Ranger.

This picture was taken at the Holdsworth Woodley factory in 1972. It shows the range of conversions on offer from Holdsworth at the time: VW campers in the foreground, Commers centre and a lone Bedford CF centre left.

Richard Holdsworth converted a wide variety of base vehicles; the Volkswagen and Commer were two of the early successes. Seen here is the Commer Holdsworth conversion looking towards the front cab. Richard Holdsworth managed to get more features into a Commer panel van conversion than many in the trade. On view here is the dinette with table (converted to double bed) and foreground bench seat, yet another bed!

into a double. The Holdsworth Sherpa could sleep any number of people from one to five. Two stretcher-style bunks were also available for fitting in the rising roof; in addition, a similar bunk could be purchased for the driving cab, bringing the total number of berths to five.

Lighting within this model came from two fluorescent fittings, one over the lounge/dinette and one over the kitchen facilities. All interior cupboards were made from real wood and treated with four coats of polyurethane varnish for protection; all interior trim to the sides of

the vehicle was fully insulated. All windows were of the polished aluminium-frame variety, with the opening versions to each side fitted with anti-theft locks. Curtains were fitted as standard to all windows, as were matching ties. Fly screens to fit the side windows were

Holdsworth furniture kits for self-fitting were extremely popular with DIY camper builders throughout the 1970s. Heather Holdsworth is seen here among a variety of cupboards, seat bases and drawers.

also available as an option. Flooring in this Sherpa was a Nairn Cushionfloor over a plywood base. As noted above, Holdsworth conversions used the Weathershield roof system – the Super-wide version of this very popular roof was fitted on the Sherpa. The roof capping was lined and insulated and the sides and ends were constructed from a nylon-reinforced PVC. Clear sections were incorporated into all sides and a coach-type ventilator was fitted into the main roof capping as standard.

From humble beginnings in the 1960s Richard Holdsworth Conversions Ltd went on to produce some very memorable motorcaravans. Many of his panel van conversions based on the Commer, Bedford CF, Transit and VW are still very popular choices on the used scene today. As time progressed the company released such models as the Holdsworth Vision and Villa based on the type 25 VW

T3 and the Holdsworth Ranger, a coach-build based on the Leyland Sherpa. The one defining point about Holdsworth models over the years was that they often dared to be different in their use of internal layouts, at a time when many used tried and trusted formulas. The company continued to prosper during the 1980s but sadly ran into financial difficulties in the 1990s with the minibus side of the business (a deal to supply several thousand minibus conversions collapsed, leaving the company with too much stock). The company eventually became Cockburn-Holdsworth for a short time, but in the end ceased trading as a motorcaravan converter. It was sad to see such an innovative company leave the ranks of motorcaravan manufacturers. It had introduced many great design ideas and achieved some memorable milestones, not least winning VW approval for its conversions. The com-

pany was also the first British company to crash-test its products, firstly with lap belts and then with fully approved three-point belts. Even bigger achievements were to follow, such as the contract to supply VW Japan with its camper requirements. The company also received VW backing to supply 6,000 VW dealers with campers throughout Europe. Today, Richard is the honorary president of the Holdsworth Owners Club, which caters for all past Holdsworth models. He now spends his time writing novels.

To conclude the details of the Holdsworth Leyland Sherpa, as the 1970s drew to a close the cost was in the region of £6,400 including VAT. A list of optional extras included a diesel engine at £470, an overdrive unit at £219, chrome bumpers £22, fridge £110, double bed kit £19, roof bunks £50 and a cab bunk £25.

19 | *Invincible Cavalier*

ABOVE: The VW Invincible Cavalier by Invincible Motor Caravan Conversions of London. It was a high-top conversion of the iconic Type 2 Volkswagen vehicle. The high top covered the entire roofline of the base vehicle and had a sliding side window fitted.

RIGHT: Identifying a factory-produced VW Cavalier is not an easy process. The company would fit the GRP high top to a customer's own van, with or without side windows, sliding and non-sliding. This would leave customers free to fit out the van as campers to their own specification.

INVINCIBLE CAVALIER – VW T2

The Invincible Cavalier based on the Volkswagen T2 is the only motorcaravan featured within this book that was not a top-selling model of the period, so why feature it? The reason is that the fantastic book written by David Eccles, *VW Camper – The Inside Story*, was such an authoritative chronicle of so many VW-based campers, I did not wish to repeat any of those models within this

publication. In fact, I had to do some stringent investigative research to find a VW camper that he had missed, hence this chapter about the Invincible Cavalier model!

Invincible Motor Caravan Conversions of Balham High Road, London, produced the Invincible Cavalier. This model certainly differed from the majority of VW campers available during the 1970s; the Cavalier was fitted with a GRP high-top roof. The model described here is

based on specifications listed for the 1976 example and based on the VW T2 delivery van fitted with the 1600cc petrol engine (a 2ltr engine was listed as an option, together with an automatic gearbox). The designer of the interior hadn't come up with any revolutionary way of setting out a VW camper living area – there is only one trusted formula for this famous rear-engine van and the Cavalier followed standard layout procedure. The one very commendable

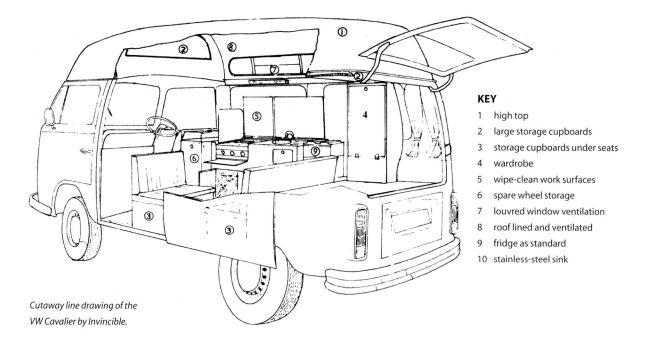

KEY

1 high top
2 large storage cupboards
3 storage cupboards under seats
4 wardrobe
5 wipe-clean work surfaces
6 spare wheel storage
7 louvred window ventilation
8 roof lined and ventilated
9 fridge as standard
10 stainless-steel sink

Cutaway line drawing of the VW Cavalier by Invincible.

feature of this VW camper was the quality of the interior. All woodwork was finished in a light oak laminate and positioning of all the facilities had been extremely well planned.

Access to this model was via the usual cab doors and sliding door on the nearside. The kitchen was located opposite the sliding door and consisted of a two-burner hob with grill and a stainless-steel sink with drainer. The sink featured a tap common to many VW models, which folded down into the sink when not in use. Cupboard space below the kitchen facilities was plentiful. Situated just below the drainer was a cutlery/utensil locker with drop-down door; under the cooker was a larger storage area where the gas bottle was stored, with the floor here being vented for safety reasons. Alongside this cupboard and below the sink was a much larger cupboard designed to store two 5gal (23ltr) water carriers. A foot-operated pump, located at the base of the kitchen unit, fed water to the sink above. Placed at the rear end of this kitchen unit (next to the drainer) was a cool box, a standard fitment on the Cavalier. A chest-type fridge could be ordered as an option and this fitted into the space occupied by the cool box. The top of the kitchen unit was complemented by a split worktop, which was finished in a hard-wearing laminate.

The living area within this model could seat three passengers, one directly behind the passenger seat (next to the side door) on a single seat, which faced

the rear of the vehicle. The other two passengers were accommodated on a two-seater bench near the rear, which faced forwards. For dining purposes, that single seat directly behind the passenger cab seat revealed a clever secret. It was unbolted from its usual position and moved forwards via a track; the bolt was then attached to another locating hole. The cushion was then lifted to reveal a hinged wooden board, which lifted over to rest flush with the seat base and then fitted on tiny ledges to the front of the kitchen cupboard. The original cushion was then replaced on the new seat's base, along with the backrest cushion, to form a comfortable

bench seat for dining. A Melamine-topped table with single leg then clipped to the kitchen unit front to complete the dining arrangements.

The bed within the living area utilized the rear bench seat and was made up by a series of plywood boards and the backrest of the seat – it was not the 'rock 'n' roll' type so often found in VW campers. Access to the cooker was not restricted when the bed was made up and ample floor space remained in order to get changed or make a drink. This was a four-berth model and two further stretcher-style bunks were housed in the high-top roof. These bunks were rolled up and kept in small ledges against the roofline

The lay-flat double bed of the VW Cavalier was situated in the traditional place for a VW model, over the engine.

when not in use. They were really only suitable for children, though, as the total length was only 5ft 5in (1,650mm). An additional child's bunk was an optional extra for the driving cab area. In addition to the storage space in the kitchen unit there was more area all around the interior. These areas included the base of the rear bench seat and the base of the single seat in the living area. Both ends of the high-top roof had very large voids in which to store the more bulky items like bedding and sleeping bags. As with most VW campers, there was of course the area behind the rear seat as a place to store yet more items. A wardrobe located in the rear had a built-in rail and was situated on the same side as the kitchen unit.

One minor annoyance on VW camper models was storage of the spare wheel. This conversion came up with a novel solution to that problem – build the wheel its own storage locker! This was directly behind the driver's seat, at the end of the kitchen, but did protrude slightly into the access space between the driver and passenger seats. Other finishing touches on the Cavalier included curtains to all windows, a

RIGHT: Invincible also carried out conversions on the Commer van. Seen here is its high-top Invincible Continental, based on the side-loading van.

BELOW: Second of the Invincible Commer models, this is the Crusader with a rising roof.

single fluorescent light over the kitchen facilities and vinyl flooring within the living area. There were small windows within the GRP high top of the metal-surround louvre type; a louvre window was also positioned over the kitchen area and all remaining windows were of the rubber seal variety.

Despite the Invincible Cavalier being very well fitted and constructed, it did have one minor fault. The GRP high-top roof only gave an interior standing height of 5ft 8½in (1,740mm), not even as good as most rising-roof options. Little wonder then that it didn't break any sales records. The cost of this model in 1976 was around £4,000 and Invincible

was also prepared to convert a customer's own van for £1,060. The company also catered for the DIY van builders and was able to supply anything from a complete kit for self-assembly to a high-top roof moulding. The Invincible Cavalier was distributed though the Catford Motor Caravan Centre.

The company responsible for the VW Invincible Cavalier also produced two conversions based on the Commer 15cwt vans. These conversions were the high-top Invincible Continental and the rising-roof Invincible Crusader. Both utilized the Commer van with side-loading/access door and placed the kitchen across the rear of the van.

ROADRANGER

20

Jennings Roadranger

Front cover of the Roadranger brochure featuring the Commer example. The Jennings, Sandbach, logo carries the words, 'Two centuries of craftsmanship'. J.H. Jennings had been coachbuilders for 200 years when the company entered the motorcaravan business in the 1960s.

JENNINGS ROADRANGER – VARIOUS CHASSIS

J.H. Jennings & Sons of Sandbach, Cheshire, had first entered the world of motorcaravan design and construction way back in the 1930s. However, as previously mentioned, this form of leisure transport fell a long way short in the popularity stakes at that time, with trailer caravans being the preferred holiday option with UK buyers. The market in the UK would have to wait until 1964 to see the next unveiling of a Jennings motorcaravan. By this time the Jennings family was celebrating the mammoth milestone of having been in the wheelwright/coachbuilding business for two centuries.

The new motorcaravan would not disappoint. There was a meeting at an inn in the Sandbach area where a discussion took place between four men.

They were all experienced in some form of commercial vehicle construction and the decision they took that day to form ERF Ltd would play a huge part in the success of J.H. Jennings throughout the 1960s and '70s. Enthusiasts of classic commercial vehicles will probably be aware that Jennings became responsible for constructing the bodywork of ERF trucks and lorries, gaining high regard for their quality finish.

By the time the 'swinging sixties' had arrived, it was the two grandsons of J.H. Jennings, Derek and Tony Jennings, who were at the head of the company. The Jennings motorcaravan was given the title Jennings Roadranger and the first example was built on the Austin 152 base vehicle. It was constructed using traditional coachbuilding skills and techniques – a hardwood frame was built, over which an aluminium skin was fitted. A one-piece GRP roof

moulding was used, which had a distinctive curve to the front section, coming down over the cab. One other notable feature of Roadranger models was the large side flashing running the whole length of the vehicle (including the cab doors), and this was always painted in a contrasting colour to the main vehicle body. Access to the Roadranger was via a single rear door, very heavy and somewhat reminiscent of the doors found on old train carriages; even the drop-down window in the top section of the door was a trait borrowed from a train carriage design. Turning attention to the interior, a prospective buyer of the period would have found this to be very familiar indeed. It was almost a carbon copy of the Paralanian model first released back in 1957, the reason being that Jennings had used the same designer and he obviously didn't see any point in

ABOVE: This period publicity picture of the Commer Roadranger was taken outside the Bears Head Hotel, Bereton Green, not far from the Sandbach factory. The exterior of this hotel was used by the Jennings Company for several Roadranger publicity shots during the 1960s; this one dates from 1969.

RIGHT: The view of the Roadranger as seen through the rear entrance door. The tall cupboard to the right housed the toilet/shower; kitchen facilities were located alongside, together with a chest of drawers. Customers had a choice of interior finish – seen here is the light oak option.

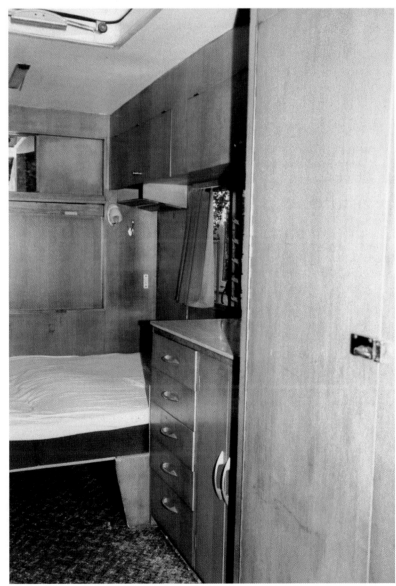

tampering with an already excellent layout.

The Jennings Roadranger was available on a variety of base vehicles, with the interior design and layout differing very little between any chassis; this chapter will therefore simply describe the interior as fitted to any of these vehicles. For the record, the Roadranger was available on the Austin 152, Commer 2500, Bedford CF (from 1969), Leyland 20 and Ford Transit.

As previously stated, the Roadranger was a coach-built model with a single-entry rear door. It was always intended as a luxury two-berth model, although child berths could be fitted as optional extras. Entering the Roadranger from the rear, one would find a toilet compartment in the right-hand corner (rear) of the vehicle, which was fitted with a full-length single door. This compartment had a roof ventilator fitted as standard, together with a single wall-mounted light. Alongside this was the sink unit, which incorporated a stainless-steel sink with drainer and a lift-up worktop faced with a laminate of wood-grain effect. To the right of the sink was a Whale hand pump for drawing water to the sink. Fresh water was housed in a 15gal (68ltr) tank stored under one of the dinette seats. A waste tank with a drain-off tap was also fitted underneath the vehicle's rear. The remainder of the sink unit consisted of a double-door cupboard with shelves

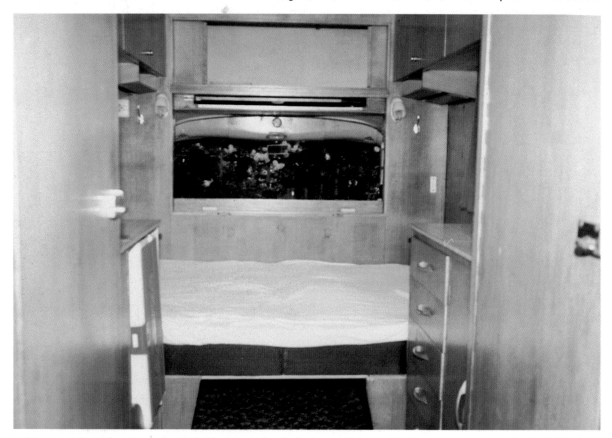

Looking towards the cab from the rear door. The bed has been made up in this picture, with the use of the dinette seats and wooden slats. The bulkhead area behind the cab has the lift-up divider on this model; other options were traditional doors or no divider at all. The table storage can also be seen here, housed in its own locker above the cab ceiling.

The stainless-steel sink/drainer with lift-up worktop. A later electrically operated tap has been fitted on this example, replacing the standard hand pump.

and a chest of five drawers next to that. Above were eye-level storage lockers with lift-up doors; these were fitted with stay-put safety catches to hold them in the open position. On the opposite side to the aforementioned toilet was a wardrobe of good size, which contained a hanging rail, storage shelf and a vanity mirror on the inside of the door.

Next to this wardrobe was the kitchen unit, which had a full cooker with oven; the oven was hidden behind twin-opening doors when not in use. The fridge was next to the cooker, but on early models this was an extra and this space was occupied by another storage cupboard, again with twin-opening doors. A worktop was to be found over both the cooker and fridge/cupboard; again this was finished in a light wood-effect laminate. A catch on the side of the wardrobe held the worktop up when the cooker was in use. As with the opposite side, eye-level storage lockers ran across over these units, extending over the dinette area.

The dinette consisted of two inward-facing seats, well upholstered with back cushions in matching fabric. The laminate-top table was housed in its own storage locker with a drop-down lid. This was located under the over-cab storage area. In a smaller locker adjacent to this

ABOVE: Shower/toilet compartment. Few were actually used as a shower, as the space was simply too confined. Most were/are used purely for the location of a chemical toilet.

BELOW: The author discovered this sad-looking Commer Roadranger some years ago; it was sitting on someone's drive being used as an extra bedroom. The owners were persuaded to part with it and it has now been restored and returned to use.

Roadrangers were built on a variety of chassis over the years, beginning with the Austin 152. This side view of a Transit example shows the delightful exterior lines of the Jennings coachwork. That distinctive side flash appeared on all models, as did the one-piece GRP roof.

was a locker housing the wooden slats, which acted as the bed base. The slats were placed in recesses along each side of the dinette seat edge and the seat bases and backs were used to form a double bed. The space above the cab was primarily for storage on the standard Roadranger, although a child's bed could be incorporated there as an option. In standard form this space was sealed with sliding wooden doors located at either side, with a vanity mirror in the centre. A single child's bed could also be ordered for the driving cab area as an option. A further option on the Roadranger was a partition between the living area and cab, which could take the form of twin doors or a full lift-up wooden panel. If the two single beds option was ordered then this panel was not available, as the beds used the cab seats for the two singles.

Aluminium-framed windows were installed on both sides of the living area (Venetian blinds were an extra for these side windows); the centre section of these was of the opening louvre type and a large roof ventilator was fitted in the centre of the vehicle. Two electric lights were fitted as standard. These were fixed to the ceiling at either end of the interior, with one switching from just inside the entrance door at the rear, the other from just behind the cab. Other notable features fitted as standard included a fire extinguisher, a 12V power socket for accessories, storage compartment for two gas bottles, a point for a gas fire and good quality floor carpet within the living area. The list of optional extras on the Roadranger model was considerable, including fly screens for windows, stabilizing jacks at the rear, individual reading lamps, gaslights, water heater and shower, chrome rear

Front view of the Transit Roadranger. The over-cab area was most useful as a storage area, but a child could sleep up there. This particular example is probably the finest surviving Roadranger in the UK and is the winner of many awards. All Roadranger models were coach-painted by craftsman using brushes, now a dying art. This one has its original factory paint finish.

ABOVE: Jennings never did advertise the fact that its Roadranger model was offered on the Leyland 20 (Standard Atlas) chassis. It must be assumed that a customer requested this particular example, as it is the only one thought to exist.

RIGHT: When the Bedford CF was introduced in 1969, it became a chassis option for the Roadranger. This survivor has been updated at some point and has had its side flashing removed.

BELOW: Although Jennings only listed the Bedford CF, Commer and Transit as Roadranger options in later years, the company was, however, prepared to build custom specials. There is a Roadranger based on the large Bedford TK chassis and a Land Rover example. This is thought to be the only Mercedes Roadranger produced to order. This picture was taken in Leamington Spa some years ago. The vehicle is still around, but now requires a major restoration.

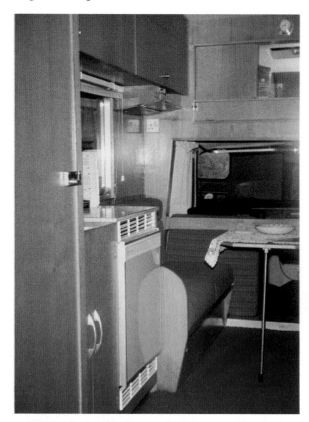

ABOVE: The Harrisons of Northants have cherished this Transit Roadranger for many years and despite getting very good use out of it, the vehicle remains a credit to them.

BELOW RIGHT: Rear of the Roadranger (Transit is seen here) with single entrance door open. The rear door on all models was similar in style to the old railway carriage doors, very heavy with the top glass section sliding down for ventilation. The roller blind at the top of the window was a standard fitment. All models featured the drop-down rear step.

This is the dark oak interior of the Leyland 20 example. The original layout for the Roadranger began life inside the early Paralanian model back in 1957. The designer later joined Jennings and took his design with him, hence the similarity. The design would turn up later inside the luxurious Tourstar model.

bumpers, wash basin in the toilet compartment and an Aeon rubber suspension system. The standard interior wood finish was sapele but an oak finish was available at extra cost.

It was noted at the beginning of the chapter which base vehicles the Roadranger was built upon, but by far the two most common were the Commer 2500 and the Ford Transit. Jennings always advertised the fact that it was willing to carry out any modifications required by customers and therefore some surviving models might differ to the description here. The company was also willing to build Roadranger models on any base vehicle specified by a customer. It is known that Jennings Roadranger examples have survived based on such vehicles as the Land Rover, Bedford TK and large Mercedes chassis. With regard to prices, and using the year 1971 as an example, the Commer was listed at £2,098, Bedford CF at £2,399 and the Transit at £2,393.

21

Kenex Carefree

One of the best publicity shots I have ever seen for a classic motorcaravan. This is the Kenex Carefree model based on the Standard Atlas,
not a publicity photograph for period swimwear!

KENEX CAREFREE – FORD THAMES 15CWT

Kenex Coachwork Ltd of Dover was a very well-established coachbuilder when it entered into motorcaravan conversions in the late 1950s. It had built an array of special bodies for such vehicles as mobile shops and fire tenders and, like so many established coachworks at that time, saw an opening for a new market when the leisure industry was expanding. The height of the company's success with regard to motorcaravan conversion came in the period from 1960–63. Around this time Kenex was taken over by the giant Martin Walter factory in Folkestone and the Kenex conversions disappeared from the listings. Conversions by Kenex were given the title Kenex Carefree, and models

were available on the Bedford CA, BMC J4, Ford Thames (10/12/15cwt) and the Standard Atlas.

Even before the Kenex company was absorbed into the Martin Walter structure, the interior of a Kenex Carefree bore many similarities to that of a Dormobile motorcaravan. The layout, furniture styling and lay-flat beds were all traits of the Dormobile, although the rising roof on the Kenex was entirely different. Viewing the interior from the twin rear doors, one found the kitchen unit to the left-hand side. This comprised a two-burner hob with grill and a sink with drainer. The entire area beneath the sink and cooker was reserved solely for storage, with twin sliding doors fitted. There was also a cutlery draw situated below the drainer. Lift-off worktops were fitted on top of the cooker and sink, as

opposed to the usual hinged variety found in most models. A combined pump/tap was placed beside the sink and water was delivered here from a 7gal (32ltr) tank housed under the vehicle floor. On the opposite side to the kitchen was a full-height wardrobe, which had a hinged mirror attached to the front of it. Next to the wardrobe was another, much smaller cupboard fitted with a drawer and a door below. On the side of the wardrobe was a gaslight and there was an additional electric light elsewhere within the vehicle. A combined seat/step had been incorporated with the base of the wardrobe; primarily used as a seat when cooking, this pulled out when required and neatly stowed away when not in use.

Four single seats were fitted in the Kenex interior, including the two cab seats. All seats were covered with PVC and finished with piping around the edges. All four seats were forward-facing for travelling. When it came to making up the beds, all seats were required, as they all lay flat. The seats on either side then butted together to form two single beds (the restricted width of the Ford Thames did not allow for transverse beds). Two full-length single stretcher bunks were housed within the rising roof, and these rolled up neatly when not in use. For dining purposes a laminate-topped table clipped to the interior wall of the vehicle, although seating four people around it, due to the seating position, was not the easiest of tasks.

Kenex Carefree based on the Ford Thames. The Dover-based converter produced some fine panel van conversions up to 1963. Dormobile then purchased the motorcaravan side of the business, but Kenex continued to build minibuses and general utility vehicles such as mobile shops.

The most popular base vehicles used by Kenex were the Atlas, Bedford CA and Thames. This beautiful Bedford CA model was well styled and had an interior to match. An Atlas Kenex can be seen in the background.

ABOVE: A familiar sight to Ford Thames enthusiasts, the rather spartan dash layout of the early Ford light commercial. The Thames was similar to the Commer in that the engine was located in the cab, between the seats.

RIGHT: Ford Thames Kenex Carefree, view through the passenger door. Thames fanatic Steve Cooper in the Midlands has restored this model. Some nice extra touches have been incorporated such as the useful toolbox/footrest in the passenger footwell.

The Thames-based Kenex had a side-loading door. Rear vinyl-covered seats are seen here; these were used in conjunction with the cab seats to make two single beds.

LEFT: Looking through the rear doors of the Thames Kenex. The traditional panel van interior layout featured cupboards to both sides and a frontal dinette. Furniture within the Kenex was a mixture of real wood, wood-grain laminate and patterned laminate to cupboard fronts. Fitments included a sink and two-burner hob with grill.

BELOW: Right-hand storage cupboards; large wardrobe and base storage with further cupboard and drawer alongside.

Hidden within the floor of the Kenex were three trapdoor panels, for the water filler, the gas-bottle storage and the battery. Floor covering was of the vinyl type. All cabinet/cupboards within the interior were finished in a hard-wearing patterned laminate with wooden edging. The Kenex interior was light and airy due to the standard fitment of windows to all sides and the rear doors. The Ford Thames also had a side-opening door that was glazed on the top half. Curtains were fitted to all windows as standard. Optional extras on this model included a vehicle heater, chrome bumpers, padded engine cover (engine was within the cab on the Ford Thames), fog lights and a radio. A fire extinguisher was a standard fitment and was situated on the side of the wardrobe near the rear doors.

One notable feature of the Kenex Carefree models that gained excellent reviews in period road tests was the full-width rising roof. It was of the type that lifted straight up by means of a metal framework, springs and pivots. It featured a GRP roof capping, which had a large amber ventilator fitted within it. The side and end panels were constructed from a strong, flexible fabric and were coloured with contrasting horizontal stripes.

Using the year 1961 as a guide for prices, the Ford Thames Kenex Carefree carried a price tag of £813. Other models were priced as follows: Bedford CA £785, BMC J4 £805 and the Standard Atlas £810. The Kenex Carefree represented good value for money as a panel van conversion back then and as

a comparison the following cars of the time were priced thus: Austin A55 Countryman £914, Ford Consul De Luxe £823, Ford Zodiac £957 and a Morris Traveller £669. Today there is a far greater price differential between panel van conversion motorcaravans and family saloon cars.

22

Land Cruiser

The beach was a favourite location for Dormobile publicity shots during the 1970s – hardly surprising given that the company was based on the south coast.

LAND CRUISER – BEDFORD CF DORMOBILE

The Land Cruiser featured here is the version first offered by Martin Walter Ltd (Dormobile). It should be noted that there were models listed under the Landcruiser name in the late 1950s and again in the early 1960s. The Dormobile Land Cruiser was first unveiled at the 1966 Earls Court Motor Show. When first released the motoring press picked up immediately on the fact that this new model bore a striking resemblance to the earlier Bedford CA Debonair body. In fact, the only real similarity between the two models was the fact that the Land Cruiser was also constructed using a one-piece GRP body. Unlike the Debonair, the Land Cruiser utilized the

The Dormobile Land Cruiser made its first appearance in the mid-1960s, based at that time on the Leyland 20 (Standard Atlas) base vehicle. Few Leyland 20-based campers remain today, although in the 1990s this particular example was a regular on the classic scene.

107

Interior of the 1968 Leyland 20 Land Cruiser. This original Land Cruiser differed greatly on the inside from the later model of the same name based on the Bedford CF.

The Dormobile sales brochure for the Bedford CF Land Cruiser. Dormobile brochures did tend to differ throughout production; this one dates from the summer of 1973. The vehicle used in this photo shoot still survives.

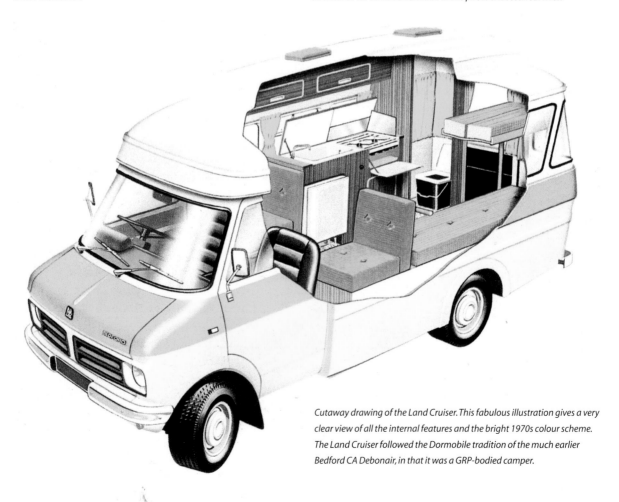

Cutaway drawing of the Land Cruiser. This fabulous illustration gives a very clear view of all the internal features and the bright 1970s colour scheme. The Land Cruiser followed the Dormobile tradition of the much earlier Bedford CA Debonair, in that it was a GRP-bodied camper.

cab of the base vehicle, in this case the Leyland 20 (formerly the Standard Atlas).

The initial Land Cruiser based on the Leyland 20 was not a great commercial success, but when the Bedford CF was released the Land Cruiser was reinvented and suddenly Dormobile had yet another very popular model on its listing. The new Bedford-based Land Cruiser was first seen at COLEX (Camping and Outdoor Leisure Exhibition) in 1971. Within a couple of years this model had become very popular, so the Bedford version of the Land Cruiser, *circa* 1973, is the one which will be described here. The Land Cruiser was based on the 22cwt CF chassis and was powered by the 2.3ltr petrol engine. This was another Dormobile model that was a one-piece GRP moulding, but it retained the metal cab of the Bedford CF. The GRP moulding did, however, run the full length of the vehicle top, front to back, with the low profile moulding over the driving cab also being of GRP material.

Entrance to the Land Cruiser was via a one-piece rear door, glazed at the top. Access to the living area was also possible through the driving cab. Viewing the interior through the rear door, there was a toilet compartment in the right-hand corner, although the toilet itself was not supplied as standard. This compartment was fitted with a bifold door, which meant that the compartment could be extended slightly when in use. The only drawback with this toilet compartment was that it had to double as the wardrobe. Situated next to this, on the same side, was the well-equipped kitchen area, which consisted of a two-burner hob with grill, with storage units below and a sink alongside the cooker. A fridge was situated below the sink, which was a standard fitment on this model. Water was pumped electrically to the sink from a 12gal (55ltr) tank mounted under the floor of the vehicle. Eye-level storage lockers were situated over the kitchen unit, but these were not repeated on the opposite side.

Opposite the kitchen and toilet compartment was a long, well-upholstered bench seat with matching backrest (the backrest was of a Pullman type and assisted with the bed set-up). This ran to a point level with the end of the fridge on the opposite side. Turning attentions to the dinette area, this was a piece of typical Dormobile ingenuity.

In addition to the two seats in the driving cab, there were two forward-facing seats directly behind these. These two seats could be altered to form two inward-facing seats for dining purposes (bench style), with the addition of a laminate-topped table. With the seating arranged in this configuration, it meant that there was in effect a length of seating running from the rear of the vehicle, to the rear of the cab passenger seat.

The sleeping arrangements once again made use of the dinette seating. The bed was formed by keeping the dining configuration, with the table forming the bed base and the back cushions then placed over the table to complete a double bed. Bunk beds were quickly made up in the rear utilizing the long seat opposite the kitchen. The Pullman-style backrest of this seat could then swing up to form the upper bunk, with the assistance of two metal tubes; a detachable safety rail was supplied for the upper bunk as standard. This clever design meant that the floor space near the kitchen was clear and the toilet was still accessible throughout the night. There was the option of a stretcher bunk for a child within the cab area. The area above the driving cab was quite large and suitable for storing large items or bedding.

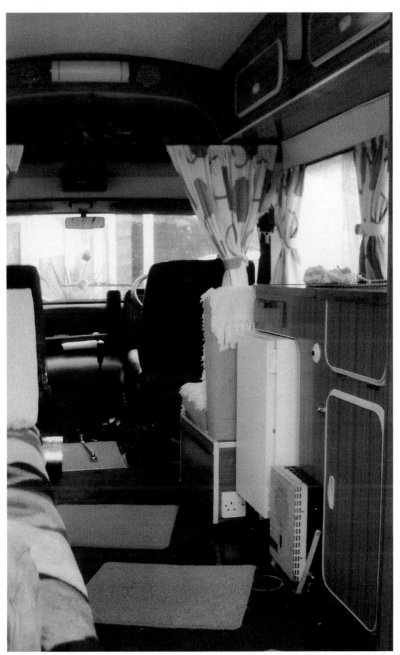

The Land Cruiser interior was extremely spacious and well thought out. The furniture and cupboards were of a wood-grain laminate finish with white plastic edging around cupboard doors and drawers.

ABOVE: *Rear view of the GRP body showing the contours to the panels, raised roofline and detailed shapes to the rear windows. The Land Cruiser was a rear-access, single-door model.*

BELOW: *Dormobile publicity picture of the Land Cruiser interior. Orange and brown were the order of the day back in 1973. The long settee seen here on the right was a clever design so typical of Dormobile. To save on floor space it converted into a twin bunk, instead of the more obvious double bed. The bunk was created with the help of several metal poles.*

Front view with the definitive lines of the Bedford CF cab. The Land Cruiser was based on the 22cwt chassis, a 2.3ltr petrol engine was fitted as standard and the 1770cc diesel unit was an optional extra. This well-kept example dates from the mid-1970s.

Additional features found in the Land Cruiser were a vanity mirror on the wardrobe door, lift-up roof ventilator, opening side and rear windows, ceiling-mounted fluorescent light, fully insulated GRP body, carpet to the cab area, vinyl flooring in the living area, curtains to all windows and provision for a gas bottle within a floor recess. The interior finish of cupboards in this model was a sapele-effect veneer laminate.

The Land Cruiser was a popular, well-equipped motorcaravan, which remains in demand on the classic scene today.

When the Land Cruiser was first released in 1971 it was priced at £1,650; by 1972 it had risen to £1,994. In the aftermath of VAT introduction in 1973, the Land Cruiser (along with all models) increased in price considerably and by 1975 the list price stood at £3,434.

ABOVE: The nameplate for the CI Motorhome was located at the base of the black window divider on the sides of the vehicle. Much like the name Dormobile, many people wrongly use the name 'motorhome' to describe a motorcaravan, when in fact it had been a model name used by CI/M since the mid-1960s. This type of confusion leads one to realize why the terms 'motorcaravan' and 'camper' are now more in vogue.

MOTORHOME – BEDFORD CF, COMMER (DODGE) AND FORD TRANSIT

The Motorhome was a name first used by Caravans International (Motorized) Ltd back in 1966, as in that year the company unveiled the Sprite Motorhome, based on the Ford Transit. That particular Motorhome ceased production in 1970 and it wasn't until 1974 that the company would once again designate the Motorhome name to one of its models. By 1974 Caravans International Ltd had become CI Autohomes Ltd and a new model appeared on its listing, the CI Motorhome MK I. This model, designed by Carl Olsen, was a development of the earlier Autohome, which was available on the Bedford CF, Commer and Ford Transit. The new Motorhome represented a departure in design and

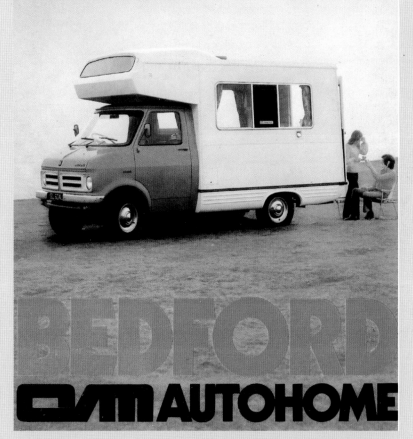

The new concept in motorcaravan design for coach-built models, the Carl Olsen-designed C/IM Autohome. This was the forerunner to the later Motorhome model. Externally it is difficult to separate the two, especially if the nameplate badges are missing from the sides!

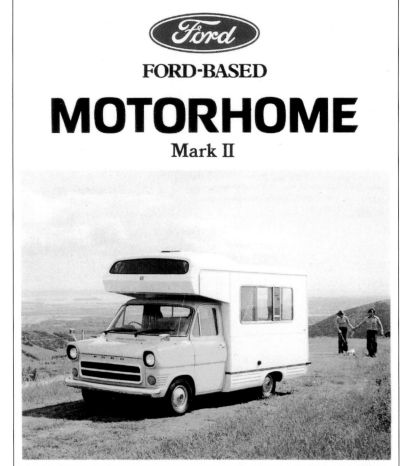

THIS PAGE:

This is the sales brochure cover of the MK II Motorhome launched in the mid-1970s. Although seen here mounted on the MK I Ford Transit chassis, the Motorhome body was also available on the Bedford CF and Commer. Note the name change of the company by this time; CI/Motorized had become CI Autohomes but remained based at the Poole factory.

OPPOSITE PAGE:

Although the MK II Motorhome body was only used on the Bedford CF, Commer and Transit, there was a slight deviation at one point. These are the distinctive lines of the Dodge Spacevan with the MK II Motorhome body attached. By 1976 the Commer name had been replaced by Dodge. At first only the name mounted on the front cab was changed, but later a plastic front grille was added. The Motorhome body, although constructed independently of the chassis, was still built using traditional methods. The sides and rear panelling were aluminium sheets; the roof section and the lower ribbed side skirts (seen here) were GRP.

build techniques to earlier coach-built examples, as the Motorhome body was constructed independently of the chassis and only mounted to the base vehicle once completed. This construction technique made better use of factory floor space, improved the build time and of course it made the export process more efficient.

The story of the CI Motorhome is one of constant change, restyling and improvements. The original MK I version of the Motorhome was simply an evolution of the very successful Autohome model, which had been released in 1971. As early as 1976 the company had already unveiled the MK II Motorhome with detailed improvements over the MK I. This chapter will begin with a look at the MK II version, concentrating solely on the Motorhome body and not the base vehicle, as the Motorhome was available on all three popular base vehicles of the period, the Bedford CF, Commer and Transit.

The Motorhome had a single rear entrance door and a combined toilet compartment/wardrobe in the rear right-hand corner (viewed looking towards the driving cab). This combined unit had a bifold door system, which allowed for the creation of an extended area when using the facilities. It was fitted with a drop-down wash basin, vanity mirror, ventilator and electric light. Alongside the toilet/wardrobe was a cupboard unit with fitted worktop; the fridge was housed in one side of this cupboard, with shelving to the other side. On the opposite side was the kitchen area and this featured a stainless-steel sink with drainer, two-burner hob and grill, together with an array of storage cupboards and drawers below. Eye-level cupboards were placed above the kitchen, giving yet more storage space. The internal layout of the Motorhome was quite traditional, with the dinette situated just behind the cab. The table, stored under the mattress in the over-cab area, could provide enough room for six people to dine in comfort.

At night-time the dinette converted into a double bed and a double child's bed was to be found in the over-cab area, with the option being that one adult could sleep in this area in place of two children. CI Autohomes did in fact fit an extension flap to the base of the over-cab bed in order to accommodate two adults, but it remained a rather confined space in which to manoeuvre. The metal safety rail placed along the outer edge of this upstairs bed doubled up as a ladder. Further features of the upper bedroom were a long window to the front, with a curtain and an electric light. An additional stretcher bunk could be ordered to fit transversely into holders across the dinette bed. There was also the option of a similar bunk for the driving cab.

Some other standard features of the Motorhome MK II included exterior access for two gas bottles in the rear, a mixture of both carpet and vinyl flooring, two fluorescent lights, on-board water tank, curtains to all windows, upholstered seating in dinette/lounge and an opening roof-mounted ventilator. All cupboards within the Motorhome were finished in a wood-effect laminate. This model was very light inside due to the good selection of both rear and side windows, with the side windows having opening panels. Towards the end of MK II Motorhome production the wardrobe (now smaller) was moved along to give 80 per cent more room in the toilet compartment. At the same time, some minor detailed changes were made to the external appearance. With regard to prices, the

The MK II Motorhome was a single-door, rear entry model with a glazed top section. The interior was conventional in its layout, featuring a centre gangway, fixtures to both sides and dinette/bed just behind the cab seats.

The finish to cupboards and panels in this model was a wood-grain-effect laminate. The kitchen units are seen here, with the optional gas fire just visible in the bottom left corner.

CI Motorhome was being listed in 1975 as: Bedford CF £2,972, Commer £2,835 and the Ford Transit at £3,180.

For 1978 the CI Motorhome was completely redesigned and was also much larger than the previous model. Although the base vehicle options remained the same, both the Ford Transit and the Commer had altered significantly. By now the MK II Ford Transit had been introduced and the Commer had been rechristened the Dodge Spacevan. In MK I and MK II variants, the CI Motorhome had been the best-selling coach-built motorcaravan throughout Europe; the launch of the MK III version would see the model hanging on to that title.

ABOVE: Storage lockers over the kitchen area. A modern light and music system has been added to this example. Roof panels were white-faced hardboard for ease of cleaning; all side, roof and end panels within the MK II Motorhome were well insulated.

Opposite the kitchen was a combined toilet/washroom in the rear corner. The wood-effect door can be seen here to the right. On the left is the fridge mounted at floor level, with another storage cupboard above.

The upholstery in this example has been replaced in recent years with a fabric similar to that in more modern campers. These seats were used for dining, with a table erected in the space between. For sleeping, both seats would fold flat to form a double bed. A further double bed was housed in the very spacious area above the driving cab, with access via a ladder supplied.

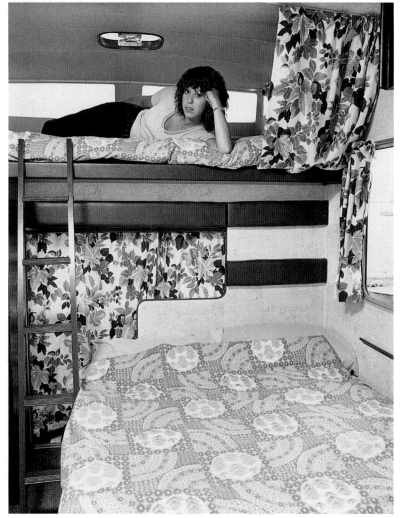

ABOVE: In 1978 the MK II CI Motorhome gave way to an all-new model, the MK III. For purposes of description it became slightly confusing, with the MK II Transit as the base and the MK III body on the back! Not quite the same problem existed with the Bedford CF and Dodge examples. The MK III remained a rear entry coach-built model and again had a huge over-cab double bed.
LEFT: Interior of the MK III Motorhome, arranged for sleeping. One double bed below, made up from the dinette area. This model is demonstrating the large bed above the cab, with access ladder in position.

The new MK III model retained the single, rear entrance door and the double bed within the over-cab area, but the internal layout had altered considerably. Looking into the interior from the rear door, the toilet compartment remained in the right-hand corner. It was fitted with a tip-up wash basin and wall-mounted cupboard as standard, the cupboard had sliding mirror doors and was fitted with a light above; both the cupboard and the sink were now of a beige colour. Situated next to the toilet, on the same side, was the dinette and table. Although these were not in the usual position directly behind the cab, they were now only to one side of the living area, leaving a walkway into the driving cab. The opposite side of the living area was the kitchen, with a wardrobe at the front end, just behind the passenger seat. Given that the kitchen took up the whole of one side interior wall, this was a very spacious design feature, which incorporated a huge worktop. Having previously owned a MK III Motorhome I can honestly say that it was one of the best interior layouts of any motorcaravan I have owned or used.

For sleeping, the dinette converted to a double bed and a further double was to be found in the over-cab area. But on this MK III model, this upper-storey bed certainly was easily capable of sleeping two adults in comfort. Optional stretcher bunks were available for both the living area (near the dinette) and in the driving cab. The whole interior of the 1978 Motorhome was typical of 1970s design and colour. All cupboards were dark brown, with sidewalls in an oatmeal shade. The worktop was in a pale yellow colour, matching the front of the fridge. All curtains and seating upholstery was a mixture of brown, gold and beige patterned colour.

The CI Motorhome in its various model designations was undoubtedly one of the great sales successes of the 1970s; it sold in huge numbers both in the UK and mainland Europe. It also remains one of the most distinctive coach-built models of the period, the MK III version in particular with its external styling and gold body colour. Prices of the MK III Motorhome in 1978 ranged from £6,273 for the Dodge version, almost £7,000 for the Bedford CF model, and over the £7,000 mark for the Ford Transit.

ABOVE: The MK III Motorhome was available in only one colour, and this is it, a subtle golden yellow. This model became one of the most popular coach-built examples of the late 1970s. Some good examples have survived, but water ingress into the section over the cab is often a problem, mainly due to seals around the windows breaking down.

RIGHT: Interior shot of the MK III Motorhome. CI Autohomes went back to the internal layout of its 1966 Sprite Motorhome for inspiration. All furniture units were located along the left-hand side and the dinette was in the exact position as in the earlier Sprite model. The toilet/washroom is just out of view in the right-hand rear corner.

24

Paralanian

ABOVE: *It is very unusual to get so many Paralanian models in one place. At this meeting of the Classic Camper Club no fewer than five examples turned up for a rally. The model in the centre is the MK II, flanked on either side by pairs of MK III models.*

LEFT: *The Paralanian coach-built model. This particular MK II example had been dry-stored for many years when discovered in the early 1990s and had fewer than 10,000 miles on the clock!*

PARALANIAN – BMC J2

The wonderfully named Paralanian will be forever regarded as one of the most luxurious motorcaravans of the immediate post-war period. The first MK I Paralanian appeared at the end of 1957. Central Garage Ltd of Bradford – a long-established dealership selling Austin vehicles – built it, really out of a necessity to diversify during the Suez Crisis of the 1950s. Its coachbuilding department didn't exactly have full order books at the time and although some of the workforce was laid off, Works Director Clifford Hobson put the remaining staff to work on two prototype vehicles – one was an ice cream sales van, the other a luxury motorcaravan. Once the motorcaravan was complete the team needed a model name for their creation and called upon the address of the factory, which was located in Parry Lane, for inspiration. Quite how the name evolved is unclear, but the address certainly did the trick and the new Paralanian was born.

As a PR exercise for the new model, a local photographer, Eric Alderton, was loaned a Paralanian for an extended trip to Athens. He made a short film (twenty minutes long) of that journey which was entitled *Overland to Athens*. It was shown on the Central Garage stand at the Motor Show in order to promote the new motorcaravan. Within a year of the MK I being released, a MK II version was announced with a slightly revised interior layout, but still built to extremely high standards. From one of the Central Garage brochures of the time, it is quite clear who the intended market for the Paralanian was; one slogan proclaimed 'If you own a Rolls you'll be proud of this too'. The prices being charged at the time were £1,050 for a standard model and £1,250 for the Deluxe. One famous customer at the time was the well-known equestrienne Pat Smythe, who owned her Paralanian for quite some time, using it as luxury accommodation when attending show-jumping events.

It is certainly worth pointing out that there were more than a few external similarities between the MK I/II Paralanian and the Bluebird Highwayman of the same period. The Highwayman was also based on the Austin 152 chassis and the likeness between the two was strikingly similar – side panels, roofline and the over-cab moulding were almost identical. It remains open to conjecture whether or not there was any copying of ideas going on, but the Highwayman was not released until a full year after the first Paralanian. Certainly there were no such arguments about the interior similarities; there were none, with the Paralanian aimed at an altogether more affluent market.

One thing is certain, this model certainly wasn't mass-produced. It was a very high-quality motorcaravan that was lovingly handcrafted using the finest materials. The main frame of the living area was constructed using ash wood, with an interior of polished walnut, and French polished by hand at that! This quality continued throughout the interior; even the floor covering was an Axminster carpet. At the Earls Court Motor Show of 1960 the Paralanian MK II was certainly at the higher end of the price bracket, being listed as £1,250, although the big Land Cruiser based on the Commer 30cwt chassis and built by Land Cruisers Ltd of London beat it to the title of 'most expensive'. The top of the range Land Cruiser was priced at £1,850, although, not surprisingly, little was ever reported about that model and I have only ever seen one survivor to date. A closer competitor to the Paralanian in the pricing stakes was the Hadrian coach-build based on the Austin 152, which was priced at £997. One surprising factor discovered from that 1960 price listing was that several panel van conversions had by then broken the £1,000 barrier (VW models by Slumberwagon and Lisburne; also the Commer–Commer diesel). In retrospect, the prices of these other vehicles made the Paralanian a very sound investment, especially given the build quality. By the end of 1961 Central Garage had released a MK III version of the Paralanian and

Interior of the dry-stored MK II. The interior was in immaculate original condition, with the cabinetmaker's sawdust still lying beneath some cupboards. It was by far the most luxurious motorcaravan available during the 1950s and this picture makes it easy to see why. The finish to the interior furniture was absolutely superb, with every grain in the real wood clearly visible.

although this model retained a similar interior layout and style, it was given a complete makeover when it came to the external styling. As this model probably sold in greater numbers than the previous two, this is the one to be described in this chapter.

As delightful as the exterior of the MK III was, it could almost be considered a step backwards towards the style of trailer caravans of the 1940s and 1950s, although it was nonetheless very appealing. The exterior coachwork had been nicely contoured and really did complement the driving cab of the Austin 152. The beautiful roofline arched from front to rear and early examples had a canvas covering. As with the previous two model designations, this MK III also had the single-entry rear door and incorporated into the body below the door was a hinged step to assist with entry. The top half of the rear door was fitted with opening louvre windows. Entering the vehicle through the rear door one found a toilet compartment in the right-hand rear corner, which was fitted with a full-height single door. This toilet compartment was also home to the gas bottles, being housed within a space at the far corner; a chemical toilet was a standard feature. Situated next to the toilet compartment was the kitchen, which was well equipped with a full oven, grill and two-burner hob. Twin-opening doors concealed the cooker when it was not in use; a hinged worktop was fitted over the hob. A small locker was built in under the cooker plinth, ideal for the storage of cooking pans. A neat chest of drawers was situated next to the cooker, the top drawer having a cutlery tray fitted as standard; this chest of drawers was topped with a small worktop.

On the opposite side of the vehicle, a full-length wardrobe mirrored the toilet compartment in the corner. The sink and drainer were next to the wardrobe and a water tap at the back was supplied from a clever tank set below the drainer. This tank was actually built around a cold cabinet made from galvanized metal and fitted with a wooden single door. Twin opening doors were fitted to a useful cupboard below the sink. A two-piece worktop added the final touches to this area, the top over the drainer hinging back and the top over the sink hinging sideways against the wardrobe side.

ABOVE: Toilet compartment of the beautiful MK II, once again real panels everywhere. A period chemical toilet completes the picture.

LEFT: The Paralanian had a full cooker with oven. Having been dry-stored for many years, the condition was quite incredible. The cooker was housed in a compartment lined with aluminium for heat protection.

Driving cab of the MK II Paralanian. Most models were based on the Austin 152 and the cab area of this model is as good as the day it left the factory. Cab seats would lay flat to form a child's bed.

BELOW: This is the MK III Paralanian, a far more distinctive shape than the earlier MK I and MK II models. The roofline was reminiscent of period trailer caravans, yet moulded nicely with the cab of the Austin 152.

Was a prettier period motorcaravan ever produced? Hard to believe that an example of this shape was only released in 1961 – it could quite easily date from much earlier times. The MK III featured a rear entry single-door with drop-down step. The rolled lower rear was an exquisite design touch, which simply added to the unique character of the Paralanian.

Side view of the MK III, clearly showing the stretched canvas roof covering.

Interior of a MK III example, though this one may well have been varnished and not polished. The dividing screen between cab and living area, a series of bifold doors, can be seen here. On the left was a clever design fixture; housed in the centre of the far cupboard was the cool cabinet. This was a galvanized cold storage unit, which had cold water around it to keep the contents cold.

Moving to the dinette, this was once again the traditional layout of inward-facing seats directly behind the driving cab; these of course converted into a double bed in the evening. There was ample storage space beneath the dinette seats. A wooden table for use when dining was housed in its own compartment within the over-cab storage area. In the bulkhead area between the living space and driving cab, the Paralanian had been fitted with wood panelling to just above table height. Bifold doors completed this panelled section, allowing light to penetrate in from the driving cab while creating an air of complete privacy in the evening. The large storage space above the cab was finished on the outside with doors and a mirror. The seats in the driving cab were of the lay-flat variety and well upholstered. By lying these down, they extended right up to the edge of the dashboard, thus creating a child's double bed or a single for an adult.

To allow light into the living area there were large windows to either side of the vehicle. These had fixed glazing at either side, with an opening central louvred section. These side windows were fitted with Venetian blinds as standard. The large bus-type roof ventilator mounted in a central position provided further light and ventilation.

Other standard fitments and features not already mentioned included a roller blind to the window on the rear door, a waste-water tank built in, full curtains to the driving cab, two electric interior lights, fully insulated double-skinned body and an exterior coach paint finish in a variety of colours. During the winter of 1961 this Paralanian MK III, based on the Austin 152 chassis, would have been priced at £1,250; a built-in bath was an extra £25! Although released initially based on the Austin chassis, it is known that examples were in fact produced based on the Commer and the Morris J2, but these were extremely limited in number. By 1964 Central Garage of Bradford had been acquired by the Looker Group of Manchester and by the mid-1960s the coachbuilding department had been closed. Spen Coachbuilders, also of Yorkshire, took over the existing orders for the Paralanian, along with all the jigs and tooling. Production by the new company recommenced in 1967, again using the J2

chassis, but also the Commer and, it is believed, the Ford Transit.

There was to be yet another twist in the Paralanian story, when the designer of the MK III, Eric Smith, began making the Tourstar model under the name of European Caravans. It is thought that some of the old Central Garage workforce was lured back for this project, which was also based in Bradford. It must be assumed that Eric Smith had the rights to his original MK III Paralanian design because the 'new' Tourstar was almost a complete replica of that MK III model, with the exception of some minor exterior changes. It was built on

the BMC J2, BMC 250JU and Commer bases. It was quite a unique situation with regard to interior design at this time; in production were the Paralanian MK III (Spen Coachbuilders), the Tourstar (European Caravans Ltd) and the Jennings Roadranger (J.H. Jennings and Sons). All three motorcaravans had near identical interiors and all three were the design of Eric Smith! It must certainly have bewildered the buyers of the time.

Of course, they do say that imitation is the sincerest form of flattery, but it is the Paralanian that is commonly regarded as the most luxurious motorcaravan of the classic period.

In addition to the luxury Paralanian, Central Garage also offered a more economical conversion on the Austin 152, the Paravan. This was a fixed-roof conversion with minimal facilities, the complete opposite of its coach-built examples. Here the combined sink/cooker is at the far end behind the cab seats, with bunk-style beds to either side. Presumably the two rear corner cupboards were for general storage, as there appears to be little else built in except for perhaps underbed/seat lockers.

25

Pitt Moto-Caravan

Peter Pitt is regarded by many as the man responsible for getting post-World War II production motorcaravans up and running. His first conversion on a VW was done out of necessity for his photographic adventures. His open-plan design became one of the most ingenious interior systems ever devised, and remained in use from the mid-1950s through to the late 1960s.

PITT MOTO-CARAVAN – VARIOUS CHASSIS

The Peter Pitt conversions were first introduced in the mid-1960s based on the VW Microbus. Peter was a German refugee based in London who required a utility vehicle for his photography business, so he set about converting a VW for his own use. This was a simple design and interior fittings were constructed with wood. The configuration of the furniture and cupboards was extremely clever, as these were designed and constructed in such a way as to allow the optimum use of the internal space. It was the forerunner to what became known as the open-plan layout. At this point there was no rising roof, the fixed van roof remaining in place.

The next turn of events is a little unclear, but Peter obviously thought that there was a market for his van conversion, bearing in mind that there were no other fully-fitted vehicles of this type around in the UK at this time. He began to market these conversions, although the cost of the VW base restricted its use, so he added the BMC J2 to the range. A Pitt conversion of the Austin 152 was taken on a road test by a member of the *Autocar* magazine team in the spring of 1959 and it certainly met with his approval. In fact, the writer of the article was extremely impressed by the fact that the table and seating could be configured into no fewer than nine different configurations, with the added bonus of the bed forming either two singles or a double. Peter really did come up with some marvellous designs at the time – the seating alone in the living area would carry up to seven people. On that particular conversion, Peter was already offering an elevating roof option at an additional cost of £90; the vehicle itself was offered at £885.

In those early years, the Pitt Moto-Caravan had yet another option, which

RIGHT: Sadly, very few pictures remain of early Peter Pitt motorcaravans, so apologies for the poor quality of this rare 1958 example. This was advertised as the 'Show around the corner', an annexe to the Motor Show held at Earls Court in 1958 and featuring campers, caravans and tents. The exhibition was held in North End Road and Peter Pitt exhibited three of his models, an Austin, VW and Ford Thames. He also introduced his first rising roof this year; this can be seen on the Ford Thames. It was widely believed by historians that he released his first rising roof around 1960, but this 1958 example appears to be a solid-sided design, unlike his later releases, which were canvas.

BELOW RIGHT: Peter's first conversions were carried out on the Volkswagens of the time, but few, if any, of those early models from over fifty years ago have survived. The majority of VW campers around today feature his open-plan layout and carry the nameplate of Canterbury-Pitt. Seen here is a Canterbury-Pitt VW interior, built by Canterbury under licence from Peter.

again centred around the roof – a 'loft' extension, which took the form of a luggage rack mounted with a tent and which was also capable of forming an extra bedroom for three children, or two adults. This roof-mounted bedroom carried a price of £59. In the infant days of UK motorcaravanning little thought appears to have been given to weight and its associated problems with regard to extra fuel consumption, unlike today where very lightweight materials are used. The Moto-Caravan was a case in point relating to this – Peter Pitt was not a man to skimp on materials, the internal woodwork being of polished oak!

BELOW: If Pitt conversions on early VW bases are rare then surviving conversions based on the Ford Thames are really in a minority. Pictured on the left here is a Thames Canterbury-Pitt from the early 1960s. This ultra-rare example is currently undergoing a nut and bolt rebuild by Thames enthusiast Steve Cooper. He also owns the delightful, and equally rare, Thames Kenex Carefree on the right.

At the Earls Court Motor Show of 1960, Peter introduced a new feature to his conversions, which certainly turned a few heads; he displayed a Sunshine elevating roof on his Ford Thames conversion. This was a spring-loaded design, which could be fully open at one end, half open, or fully closed all round. The sides of the roof were in two sections and control was via adjustable strings at one end. The new roof was offered on all the Moto-Caravan models of the time, including Austin, Commer, Morris and Ford Thames. Two sleeping berths were located within the extra roof space, bringing the total number of berths to six. The fixed roof option remained on the model list at this point, together with the loft bedroom.

In 1962, a summary in *Autocar* stated, 'We are sorry to learn that Peter Pitt, well-known character in motor caravanning, is no longer working in this field, but his design is still available from Canterbury Sidecar.' In truth, Peter had granted this company a licence to build motorcaravans using his open-plan design. The models were still listed as the Pitt Moto-Caravan, but were now sold by Canterbury Sidecars of Romford, Essex. Yet another new feature had been added to the range by 1962, the option of a GRP high-top roof, but, as with a similar option by Cotswold at the time, the public was not quite ready for high-top models. Moving forwards only two years, the company offering the Moto-Caravan conversions had become Canterbury Industrial Products (Aveley) Ltd. In the buyers guides of 1964 the base-vehicle range had changed slightly; no longer listed were Austin, Commer or Morris. The Ford Thames remained an option, but the VW Kombi, Microbus and Microbus Deluxe were now the favoured base vehicles. Prices had also increased by this time, so much so in fact that the VW Moto-Caravan, based on the deluxe chassis and fitted with a rising roof, retailed at £1,236. This was even more expensive than the luxury coach-built Paralanian, which was priced at £1,025 in the same listing. Today, this price comparison appears somewhat strange, given the two models in question – a VW Moto-Caravan in superb condition is currently likely to sell for a five-figure sum, but a Paralanian (despite its luxury) would struggle to command such a high figure.

The famous Pitt open-plan layout, so-called because the interior fitments could be altered to suit the user. It was obviously popular with buyers as it remained in production throughout the 1960s on both the Thames and later the Transit.

The vast majority of surviving Pitt Moto-Caravans do tend to be based on the VW, rather than Austin, Commer, Morris or Ford Thames. Whether that is because more models were built on the VW is unclear, as no build records remain. It could also be that there are numerous survivors out there on other chassis, with the current owners being unaware of what the conversion is; this has often proved to be the case with various other conversions.

Peter Pitt sadly passed away in 1969. According to people who knew him, he remained just a little 'miffed' that he didn't quite get the recognition that he believed he deserved for his contribution to the development of motorcaravanning in the UK. Thankfully, I believe that this situation has now been rectified with the recent rapid growth in interest in classic motorcaravans. The licensing agreement that Peter had with Canterbury expired upon his death; the following year the company reappeared simply as CIP Ltd and the Pitt name had disappeared.

By 1960 Peter Pitt had graduated from a stand within the marquee around the corner and moved into the Motor Show proper, stand number 94 according to this advertisement. Seen in this period piece is an Austin 152 fitted with the Pitt sunshine roof. As Pitt only released this roof in 1960, it is quite possible that it fooled historians into believing it was the first Pitt rising roof. Many journalists at the time reported: 'At last, the rising roof has arrived on Pitt conversions.' Those journalists were obviously not around in 1958!

26

Romany

This is a much later Romany model, identified by the deeper Bedford windscreen. Very early Dormobile Caravans had the split windscreens, later a one-piece small screen. Seen here is the last version before production ceased.

ROMANY – BEDFORD CA

The Romany is quite possibly *the* item from the classic years of UK motor-caravanning, having become such an iconic image. That candy-stripe canvas roof, hinged high in the air from one side of the vehicle, really conjures up an image of camping long ago – I am of course referring to the famous patented Dormobile rising roof as fitted to many Dormobile models from the mid-1950s. In the raised position one knew instantly, even from a great distance, that it must be a Dormobile motorcaravan. Although it wasn't the first rising roof to be fitted to a conversion (that honour went to Calthorpe), it certainly became the enduring image

of 1950s' and 1960s' campsites around the UK.

The first Martin Walter motorcaravan to be fitted with the roof was the Dormobile Caravan, a conversion of the popular Bedford CA. This was the model that would put the names of both Martin Walter Ltd and Dormobile well and truly on the map. The company already had a utility vehicle in production based on the Bedford CA. It featured the famous Dormatic seats that could be altered into several positions and, in addition, be laid flat to form a bed. Once some simple interior fittings and the rising roof were added, it became a motorcaravan. But even the Martin Walter Company must have been a little surprised at the instant success of its cre-

ation, which quickly gained rave reviews in the motoring press, not least because it was pitched at an affordable price. It was also helped considerably by the fact that it was based upon the most popular light van of the time, the CA. In this period of post-war UK history, people were once again beginning to take part in leisure activities on a greater scale, so the launch of the Dormobile Caravan fitted perfectly with the growth of the economy; the two went hand in hand and a legend was born.

To this day, those early models remain very pleasing to look at, with their round porthole window in the side and the small version of that famous roof. Throughout the early 1950s, the company kept the price of this model to an

RIGHT: Early sales brochure cover for the famous Dormobile caravan. This is a very early model with the round porthole side window and small rising roof. This is the camper that introduced many people to the world of motorcaravanning during the 1950s.

LEFT: With some minor restyling, no porthole window and a larger rising roof, the Dormobile Caravan became the Bedford Romany. That side-hinged roof with its candy stripe fabric became a well-known sight around campsites during the 1960s.

BELOW: The two flagship models of the Dormobile range during the 1960s, Debonair on the left and Romany on the right.

absolute minimum in order to maximize sales – it was one of the lowest priced models on the annual listings. In 1958 (in standard form) the cost of a Dormobile Caravan was £725, beating its two nearest rivals, the Calthorpe Home Cruiser and the Pitt Moto-Caravan, by some margin. The giant Martin Walter concern did, of course, have a head start on its rivals during the 1950s, as it was already a well-established coachbuilders with huge factory premises and a trained workforce. Add to these factors the company's long-standing relationship with Vauxhall Motors, and you have a recipe for undoubted success, as long as you have the goods to market in the first instance, and Martin Walter certainly did. In terms of sales, the Dormobile Caravan left all other UK models trailing in its wake; it really was in a league of its own. In fact, such was the demand for Martin Walter Bedford CA conversions (both the Utility van and Dormobile Caravan) that base vehicles were transported by a direct rail

link from Luton (Vauxhall) to the Martin Walter factory in Folkestone. One figure certainly worth stating here concerns Bedford CA conversions by the company in 1959; in that year alone it produced 10,000 Bedford CA conversions, which included the Dormobile Caravan, Utilabrake, Utilicon, Utilabus and Workobus.

As the 1960s dawned, the famous Dormobile rising roof had by now been enlarged and the Dormobile Caravan was now the Romany range. By the time the company put on its display at that year's Motor Show, its model line-up numbered fifteen examples on six different base vehicles. But despite extending its range of models, the Romany range remained the favourite with buyers. The Romany range actually consisted of five different options. Firstly, there was the Romany Standard, which was a Bedford CAS (short wheelbase model) with a fixed factory metal roof. Next came the Romany Super, again on the Bedford CAS model, but

this time fitted with a rising roof. These two models were then duplicated, but this time on the Bedford CAL (long wheelbase model). The top of the Romany range was the De Luxe, based on the Bedford CAL; this model had both a rising roof and a roof rack built onto the frontal roof area. This gave a very sleek and streamlined appearance. Adding to the delightful external appearance of the De Luxe model were GRP tail fins fitted on the rear sides of the vehicle. This Romany range in 1964 stretched in price from £658 for the Standard through to £888 for the De Luxe. As if this Romany range wasn't confusing enough, another Bedford CA model was offered at £995; this was the Deauville. It had most of the features found in and on the De Luxe offering, but the interior was finished in real wood, as opposed to the laminate-faced cupboards of the other models.

Throughout the 1960s the Dormobile Romany continued to be the biggest

Rear view of the Romany with roof closed. First introduced in 1952, the Bedford CA became a huge favourite with light commercial users from day one. Martin Walter Ltd not only carried out motorcaravan conversions on the CA but also many utility vehicles. None was more popular than the Dormobile camper.

Interior of the Romany looking towards the rear. Even when closed, the large roof windows gave plenty of light into the vehicle. The kitchen can be seen on the right, with the wardrobe on the left.

These particular seats have been recovered at some point, as the originals had a vinyl covering. The Dormatic seats were a design success for the Folkestone company, as their ingenious mechanism allowed them to be altered into a variety of positions, both as seats and beds.

ABOVE: The unmistakable view of the Bedford CA cab. Driving with the sliding doors open during a hot summer was a firm favourite, but probably not politically correct today! Dashboard was sparse yet functional; gear change was column-mounted.

RIGHT: This is the interior of the top of the range Romany, given the title Deauville. This featured a full wooden interior of excellent quality and finish. The exterior was also treated to an assortment of goodies, including GRP tail fins and rear louvre windows.

selling panel van conversion in the UK. The model name was eventually carried over to the Bedford CF when it replaced the CA in 1969.

For purposes of description, this chapter will concentrate on the Bedford CA Romany from 1967, as by this point there had been considerable changes from the early example. The Romany was a four-door model featuring sliding cab doors and twin opening rear doors. With the exception of the Dormatic seats and their variable positioning, the interior was of the traditional panel van layout. Looking towards the cab from the rear, there was a kitchen on the left fitted with a sink, two-burner hob with grill, drawer and storage cupboards below. A water carrier was situated on the end, nearest the rear doors, and this supplied water to the sink via a hand pump. On the opposite side to the kitchen was a wardrobe and further storage unit. The base of the wardrobe incorporated a pull-out stool/seat for use when cooking. All units in the Romany Standard and Super models were of a light wood-effect laminate.

Fitted along both vehicle sides were long windows with sliding panels; a Dormobile air-scoop window was placed near the cooker to aid the expulsion of cooking smells and condensation.

The forward dinette/seating area was centred on the famous Dormatic seats, which were capable of being turned every which way imaginable. Not only could they face forwards and reverse, it was also possible to fold them up completely against the vehicle sides in order to carry bulky items. At night, these seats could be altered to

ABOVE: It's strange how old campers seem to attract young people – their penchant for the older VW models is legendary. These days, the popularity of other campers is catching on fast and the Dormobile Romany is high on the list.

BELOW; Front view of the Romany, with side-hinged roof in the raised position.

form either two single beds or one double. Two stretcher bunks were housed within the cavernous rising roof. The floor covering in the Romany range differed between each model, with linoleum, rubber and PVC coverings being used. The two gas cylinders were housed within special compartments in the vehicle floor. A metal container was also housed in the floor and this could either be used for further storage or a chemical toilet.

The large, side-hinged Dormobile rising roof gave ample standing room within the vehicle. It was fitted with roof lights/ventilators. Curtains were fitted as standard to all windows; electric lighting was another standard fitment. The optional extras available for the Romany were quite exhaustive, as one would expect from Dormobile, but as with most panel van conversions of the period, the list did include a fridge. Prices for the Romany in 1967 had risen to £872 for the Super model and £947 for the De Luxe. Due to the large numbers produced over a significant time span, many examples have survived.

Sprite Motorhome

27

The Sprite Motorhome by CI/Motorized of Poole. A little over a hundred examples were produced between 1966 and 1970. Ford worked closely with CI/M to supply a slightly longer chassis for this spacious coach-built model.

SPRITE MOTORHOME – FORD TRANSIT

The Sprite Motorhome was launched in 1966, a coach-built conversion that was only available on the Ford Transit chassis. This model was a collaboration between Ford and Caravans International (Motorized) Ltd, as Ford supplied a specially extended chassis to suit the new coach-built model. The Sprite Motorhome was in fact based on an extended version of the LWB, 25cwt Custom Transit, powered by the 2ltr OHV (1996cc) petrol engine. Ex-CI/M employees once informed me that certainly no more than one hundred Sprite Motorhomes were ever built. This was due (in their opinion) to the fact that it was an uneconomical model to build and money was lost on every model sold.

The whole Caravans International (Motorized) division grew from the giant Bluebird Caravans empire, which included the Sprite name. The external lines of the Sprite Motorhome owed much to its caravan pedigree; in fact, had the Transit cab not been there and the body lines been allowed to form a complete living unit, then it could easily have been designed as a trailer caravan. It was a point picked up on by the motoring press of the period, some enthusing about its beauty and others deeming it unattractive. Such a scenario faces many people when confronted by a motorcaravan of the classic period – some are instantly smitten by the external looks of a vehicle, whereas others may consider it quite hideous. For the record, the Sprite Motorhome remains one of my all-time favourite motorcaravans and, having owned one, I still hold that view. The internal design worked in every way for my family and to me the external lines are almost an art form, but beauty, as

they say, is in the eye of the beholder. This model was produced between 1966 and 1970, but in 1968 the internal layout was altered slightly and the materials used were changed from ash panelling to a wood-effect laminate finish. One can only assume that build time and costs had a part to play in that decision.

Focus here will be on the earlier model, as, in my opinion, it had a better seating/dining layout and a more attractive finish to the internal surfaces. Externally, both early and later models remained the same. Entrance to the living area was through a delightful curved single door situated on the side of the vehicle, near the rear. A fold-down step incorporated into the base of the door area aided entry. Upon entry, one had a low slimline cupboard containing useful storage shelves and smaller lockers fitted under the large rear window. Immediately ahead, in the

ABOVE: *The author owned this 1967 example for a period during the 1990s. He considers it to be one of the best classic coach-built examples, with a brilliant internal layout. Sadly, the quality of finish never did match the design expertise. For the record, a Ford Thames Kenex Carefree is parked alongside.*

LEFT: *Rear view of the Sprite. The side entrance door left the rear panel free for the fitting of a modern bike carrier. The large window was in the rear of the living area, while the smaller window was located in the shower/toilet compartment. Chrome rear bumpers add a touch of classic status.*

RIGHT: *The location of the dinette/seating was excellent, directly behind the driver's seat. This left a good access gangway down the length of the vehicle. The dinette did, of course, form the double bed when laid flat.*
BELOW RIGHT: *The side entrance door was beautifully shaped, giving access into the rear section via a drop-down step.*

rear corner, was a combined toilet/ shower compartment. This was lined in a waterproof finish of tile effect and was pink in colour. A raised plinth was provided for a chemical toilet and an electrically operated shower was fixed to the rear end wall. The shower utilized a system of filling the sink with hot water and then pumping it around to the shower. Situated next to this shower compartment was a slim wardrobe and a further storage cupboard/locker; both had shelves fitted above.

On the interior wall where the entrance door was placed were the excellent kitchen facilities. The kitchen comprised a two-burner hob with grill and full oven, stainless-steel sink and drainer with water pumped to the sink via a foot-operated switch. A 10gal (46ltr) underfloor water tank was fitted as standard. The sink/drainer unit had large storage facilities beneath with twin doors. A substantial crockery/food storage unit completed the kitchen with a very large (gas only) fridge below. Yet another storage cupboard was placed just behind the passenger cab seat. At eye level in the Sprite there were not the usual cupboards as found in most conversions, but long slender windows on each vehicle side, both with opening sections.

One of my favourite Sprite features was the design of the dinette. It seated four people on bench-style cushions around a table of good proportions. These seats were arranged with one

LEFT: The rear of the Sprite shows the rectangular window with storage shelf above. The cupboard space was below, with the toilet/shower to the left-hand corner. The cooker with oven is visible in the bottom right-hand corner.

BELOW: Storage within the Sprite was simply cavernous. Here is a large unit above the fridge, which had a lift-up front and fitted shelves.

bench seat facing the rear of the vehicle and one facing towards the front. It was to be found directly behind the driver's seat, on the same side of the vehicle as the shower/toilet. The placement of the dinette in this way kept the main thoroughfare from front to rear clear for walking. On later models the dinette was placed in the more traditional area behind the cab with seats facing inwards. The area above the driving cab was a child's bed, with two additional stretcher bunks supplied for the living area. These were rolled up and stored against the internal sides when not in use. When required for sleeping, they were pulled out and quickly constructed using the support bars provided, meaning that the Sprite was a full five-berth model, though in reality it was more suited to two adults and three children.

The remaining standard features of the Sprite Motorhome included internal electric lights, a large roof ventilator, vinyl floor covering, curtains to all windows and a fully insulated body.

In the left of this picture the worktop is over the cooker. Next to this is the sink with two waterspouts just visible. One of these supplied water to the sink, the other was piped to the shower – yes, you filled the sink with hot water, adjusted the spout into the sink and jumped in the shower; crazy, yet ingenious!

Here is the original shower, located at the rear corner of the vehicle. The pink tiled hardboard was the standard finish for the Sprite shower; the toilet is a more modern replacement.

One minor drawback with this model was difficulty of access from the living area to the cab, or vice versa – this was because a double passenger seat was fitted as standard, although some owners solved the problem by replacing the double seat with a single one. The price of the Sprite in 1967 was £1,522; the optional fridge was an additional £39. This model gained excellent reviews in period road-test reports, not least because of the use of the space within the living area and the high level of standard equipment. It continues to have a loyal band of followers, although it is believed that fewer than thirty of the original one hundred models have survived.

Production of the Sprite Motorhome came to an end in 1970, with the Transit Landliner replacing it.

RIGHT: *Another view of the shower, but this time the tall storage cupboard alongside and the smaller cupboard are both visible.*
BELOW: *According to ex-CI/M employees, the Sprite Motorhome was too costly to produce and had not been priced accordingly. This model, the Landliner, replaced the Sprite Motorhome. Again, this was a coach-built example, although this model had a rear entrance door.*

28

Sun-Tor

The prototype BMC Sun-Tor by Torcars of Devon. This press picture dates from December 1968. Torcars used the BMC ½ ton van as the base for its small conversion, as it appealed to couples who wanted to garage their camper.

SUN-TOR – MORRIS MARINA (AND OTHER CHASSIS)

Torcars of Torrington, Devon, will always be remembered within motorcaravanning spheres as the company that managed to squeeze a quart into a pint pot with its excellent micro-campers. These little two-person campers, firstly on the BMC half-ton van and later on the Leyland Marina, were market leaders in their class throughout the 1970s.

The first prototype Sun-Tor was unveiled to the public in 1968. This was an ingenious design based on the small BMC half-ton van. Despite its limited dimensions, the designers had managed to fit all the necessary facilities inside, including a cooker, sink, cupboards, double bed, dining tables and, of course, a rising roof. But not only had they fitted all these attributes within such a confined space, they had achieved a very high level of workmanship. The Torcars company was the brainchild of two partners, long-time motorcaravanner Alan Hutchinson and Ronald Webster

of Webster Conversions. Carrying out conversions on smaller vans was certainly nothing new – the Dormobile Roma based on the Bedford HA and the Mini Wildgoose, based upon a Mini van, were already in production when the Sun-Tor was launched. But the two factors already mentioned, quality and design, made the Sun-Tor an instant success with buyers.

Torcars was also rather unique in its approach to the sale of its conversions; unlike other companies, it did not use sales distributors around the UK, preferring instead to sell directly from its factory in Torrington, Devon. There was a small campsite attached to the factory set-up to allow buyers to try out their new acquisition from the outset. By the early 1970s, Torcars had added a panel van conversion of the Commer to its line-up, again with a rising roof. As the decade developed, more models were introduced, including conversions on the Leyland Sherpa (panel van and coach-build), a high-top conversion on the Commer and in 1972 the introduction of the

company's best-selling model, the Marina Sun-Tor. In fact, the Torrington company was prepared to carry out special orders on any base vehicle to a customer's requirements.

Despite mediocre success of the other models in the range, it would be the Marina Sun-Tor that really catapulted the company into the motorcaravan hall of fame. The Marina Sun-Tor was constantly modified and improved through its production run, but this chapter's description will be of the model as it was in 1974.

There were quite obvious advantages and disadvantages to a micro-camper of the Marina van size. The most blatant minus point was its rather limited dimensions and owners reported that it was best used as a step up from tenting and as a picnic vehicle. A big plus point, though, was that it was small enough to fit in the average family garage. As an aid to its limited dimensions when camping, extra awnings were available at the time that attached to the rear, giving the occupants more

The Sun-Tor Register holds a number of rallies around the UK each year for surviving examples of all Torcars campers.

This is a Morris version of the BMC conversion. The tall rising roof is a most notable feature of the Sun-Tor. In order to enjoy a prolonged camping foray, the attachment of a rear annexe was advisable.

space. Based on the Morris Marina van fitted with a 1275cc petrol engine, the Sun-Tor retained the factory-fitted twin opening rear doors.

ABOVE: When production of the BMC van came to an end Torcars turned its attention to conversions based on the new Marina van. An early example is seen here with the roof raised.

When looking in from the rear, the interior was the conventional layout of facilities attached to either interior side, but all in miniature. Immediately to the left was the small cooker with a two-burner hob and grill, which was mounted into a small wooden cupboard with a locker below. This cooker unit was fitted with a lift-up worktop. Alongside the cooker was a sink, again with a lifting worktop and a tap, which pumped water from a container housed under the seat, was fitted to the side. The sink was housed in a slimline cupboard that was set back slightly from the cooker unit. Below the sink were storage cupboards fitted with sliding doors. Further slimline lockers were fitted above the kitchen units (though not at eye level in this model, more like waist level when standing!), and a fluorescent strip light was attached to the underside of these higher lockers. At the end of the sink unit was a further cupboard (recessed yet further in from the sink unit) and this housed the gas bottle. The gas storage cupboard was not fitted with a conventional door, but with a flap that acted as one of the two dining tables (more on the dining facilities shortly).

Interior of the Marina Sun-Tor. Torcars made excellent use of such a confined space and the quality of the interior furniture was of a very high standard. Using the sink and cooker was best done sitting on the stool provided. Front and rear seats folded flat to form a double of restricted dimensions; optional stretcher bunks could be ordered for the roof space if you were feeling adventurous!

Turning attention to the opposite side of the interior, there was a small (everything was small on this conversion) wardrobe facing the cooker. About three or four clothes hangers would fit in here, with just enough drop for a shirt or jacket; a couple of pairs of shoes would fit in the base. Fitted at the base of the wardrobe was a flap that could swing out and this acted as a stool when using the cooker opposite. Running alongside the wardrobe was a unit that mirrored the unit on the opposite side, minus the sink. This provided further useful storage area and was again fitted with sliding doors. At the end of this

A later Marina on the left with revised front grille. On the right is a Leyland Sherpa panel van conversion with rising roof.

unit was another cupboard for gas-bottle storage, and this was fitted with the second of the two table flaps. An added bonus at the rear of the vehicle was thin lockers, fitted with a shelf and sliding doors, which were built onto the inner rear doors. The finish within the interior was of real wood to all cabinets and laminate for the doors, the overall effect of which was very pleasant.

The factory-fitted seats in the Marina had been replaced with those of Torcar design. These well-upholstered seats replaced the driver and passenger seats and were able to convert from forward-facing to rear-facing. In the rear-facing mode they were used in conjunction with the drop-flap tables for dining. The Marina Sun-Tor was also fitted with rear seats, which, when folded flat and combined with the front seats, formed the double bed – although there would always be one unlucky person who had the steering wheel protruding into their sleeping space! The rising roof on this model (and the previous BMC half-ton van model) gave full standing height within the vehicle. It had a roof capping of GRP material and flexible side and end walls. The whole roof was constructed

As the 1970s progressed, Torcars went from strength to strength. In addition to the popular Marina Sun-Tor, the company was also converting the Leyland Sherpa and the Commer seen here. This is the Commer Sun-Tor Major, with rising roof and side entry door.

around a metal framework, which swung up with the minimum of effort. The roof capping was held down to the van roof by means of strong clips when travelling.

The list price for a Marina Sun-Tor in 1974 was £1,722, which included a fire extinguisher and first-aid kit. Optional extras included a stretcher bunk in the roof at £7.50, a rear awning at £53, cool box £3.95 and mud flaps for £4.90. The Marina Sun-Tor should not be confused with the Suncamper Marina that was also available. This was a slightly different model and did not have a rising roof, but it was still made by Torcars. In its class (micro-camper) the Marina Sun-Tor was certainly the best selling model. A series of company takeovers and management changes saw the Sun-Tor name finally end up in the hands of a motorcaravan dealer in the Midlands, which for a period produced another version of the Sun-Tor on both the Marina and the later Morris Ital. That version, however, featured a side-hinged rising roof in place of the straight-up original.

One strange fact to note about the Marina model is that despite its long production run, more examples of the Torcars conversions on the BMC half-ton van are thought to have survived, which seems at odds with the fact that the latter was only in full production for just under four years. It is very likely that this has occurred due to the poor gauge of metal used on Marina models combined with ineffective rust-proofing from new. I'm sure that owners of all Marina models in the range would testify to severe rust problems around front wing areas and wheel arches!

ABOVE: It has to be one of the most unusual high-top roofs ever built. This is the Commer Hi-Tor by Torcars. The rear section of the GRP roof was fitted with clear plastic and had sunblinds fitted on the inside.

RIGHT: Not a company to rest on its laurels, Torcars turned its attention to the Toyota Hiace van in the mid-1970s. Pictured here is the Sun-Tor Hiace with rising roof.

29

Travelhome

The MK III Travelhome by CI Autohomes was based on the MK II Ford Transit chassis. This was the larger sister vehicle to the other CI coach-built model, the Motorhome.

TRAVELHOME – FORD TRANSIT

The Ford Transit Travelhome was the larger stablemate of the Motorhome by CI Autohomes of Poole, Dorset. The first Travelhome was released in 1975 based on the Transit 130 Custom chassis and powered by the 2ltr petrol engine, a 3ltr unit being an option at the time. The Travelhome was another motorcaravan from CI Autohomes designed by automotive designer Carl Olsen. Upon its release, the new Travelhome was greeted with great enthusiasm by the motoring press, some hailing it as a lavish American-style camper with European specifications. This was hardly surprising, as Carl Olsen was actually a young American. The Travelhome was unveiled at a special press conference at the Poole factory; the large London motorcaravan dealers, Wilsons Motor Caravan Centre, were

obviously impressed with the new luxury model, as they immediately placed an order for £45,000. It wasn't just the press who were impressed with the Travelhome – celebrities of the time who purchased one included 'Sooty and Sweep' creator Harry Corbett and radio and TV personality Sir Jimmy Saville OBE.

Luxurious and well-fitted the Travelhome may have been, but in reality it was really a bigger and better version of the already popular Autohome/ Motorhome model. The family likeness, even externally, was very apparent. This coach-built model had a single-entry rear door with a large glazed section to aid reversing and a large window to each side; these side windows were double-glazed. Additional long slender windows were placed at the rear, just below the roofline. The one-piece GRP roof was fitted with both small and larger ventilators and had a long window

fitted in the over-cab section at the front. The sides and rear of this coach-built example were an aluminium skin over a softwood frame; glass-fibre insulation was sandwiched between the aluminium and the inner hardboard panels. Upon entering the Travelhome through the rear door, one was greeted with a familiar layout of furniture along each internal wall and a dinette/lounge behind the driving cab, although in this model the dinette was divided from the cab by single wardrobes.

When entering the vehicle, in the rear right-hand corner was the fridge with a set of storage drawers alongside. A worktop of wood-grain laminate topped these two fixtures. Next to the set of drawers was the cooker, which had the ubiquitous two-burner hob but also an oven fitted as standard equipment. A lift-up worktop over the cooker completed the units. More storage in

The early Travelhome was based on the MK I Ford Transit. It was a large coach-build with rear entry door, big sliding windows in the sides and had a huge double bed over the cab area.

the kitchen area was supplied via eye-level lockers with sliding doors. In the opposite corner to the fridge was a spacious toilet/shower compartment. This housed a shower unit and tray, bathroom cabinet, washbasin and chemical toilet. This compartment was lined with a waterproof vinyl. The stainless-steel sink was situated next to the shower compartment, with a hot-water boiler fixed to the side of the shower sidewall. The placement of this boiler was quite logical in order to supply hot water to both the sink and shower. A further storage unit was to be found below the sink.

The dinette/lounge occupied the position just behind the driving cab, but

Early Travelhome again, this time viewed from the right front. The roof was of a bulbous shape over the cab in order to accommodate the double bed; this area also had a one-piece long window. The bull-nose front on this Transit indicates that a 3ltr petrol engine or diesel unit was fitted.

LEFT: The kitchen area within the Travelhome MK III was in the rear right-hand corner. It was a very well-designed area with all standard fittings such as fridge, cooker and hot water heater. The kitchen was an L-shape and had an abundance of storage units and drawers.

with a slight difference. Immediately behind both the driver and passenger seats were single wardrobes, which were fitted with shelves and hanging rails. The base of one of them housed the gas bottles. Sandwiched between the rear units and the single wardrobes was the dinette. For dining purposes the dinette seats could be arranged to form two inward-facing bench seats, with a table in-between. For travelling, these seats could be altered to form two forward-facing seats. The wardrobes that would then be facing the rear occupants had been cleverly angled so as not to restrict the forward view. The Travelhome had a spacious over-cab sleeping area with deep mattresses. This upper bedroom was fitted with an

BELOW: Don't you just love these period press pictures? In this one the woman is standing in the space between the kitchen and the rear toilet/shower compartment. All interior furniture in the Travelhome MK III was a very dark wood-grain finish.

electric light and could be curtained off at night. Three electric strip lights were fitted as standard in the living area and this was one of the first models to be fitted with a dual battery system as standard, so as not to flatten the vehicle battery when camping. Another feature of the luxury Travelhome was the addition of a thermostatically controlled central-heating system.

The Travelhome price when launched in 1975 was a whopping £4,500. Despite this hefty price tag, the Travelhome MK I was a big success. In fact, during its development from MK I through to MK IV, it had a very loyal customer base and in its various guises sold well not only in the UK but also on the continent.

As with the CI Motorhome of the same period, the Travelhome was only available in this distinctive gold colour scheme. In retrospect it was well chosen as the white roof and cab of the Transit matched the gold extremely well and in fact these models don't look out of place today among their modern counterparts.

Dinette seating was divided between each side of the Travelhome. One dinette seated two people and the other seated four. Simple addition means that the four-person dinette converted into a double bed and the two-person into a single.

30

Wildgoose

*The Goodwin family of Lincolnshire own one of the best examples in the UK, a five-berth example resplendent in blue and white livery.
It is seen here from the rear with the front-hinged roof in the raised position. Yes, entry really was via that small door at the rear!*

WILDGOOSE – BMC MINI

It is open to debate whether a motorcaravan produced in numbers of fewer than seventy should be included in a book based upon the most popular models of the classic period. But the Wildgoose was no ordinary motorcaravan and a BMC Mini was not one of the usual base vehicles. The launch of the Mini Wildgoose in the latter part of 1963 rather took the motoring press by surprise, as they were a little uncertain as to what to say about this rather strange concept. It was unlike anything that had gone before and was released at a time when the Austin 152, Bedford CA and Commer were the expected base vehicles for conversion to motor-

caravans. In retrospect, the concept does take some getting used to. We are now well aware that in several polls in the UK the Mini was voted car of the century and was certainly the trendiest thing to be seen driving during the 'swinging sixties'. But this Wildgoose camper creation was released less than four years after the Mini itself was first unveiled! Hardly surprising therefore that it caused such a stir.

The Wildgoose was the creation of a coachbuilding company based in Wiston Avenue, Worthing, and the Managing Director at the time was one Mr Bennett, himself a motorcaravanner. The initial philosophy of the company was that the Wildgoose should be marketed as a multi-purpose family estate car, with

the useful benefit of it being possible to use it for occasional camping.

The Wildgoose was a coach-built example in every sense – the converters took a basic Mini van, then removed everything from the back of the driving cab. They then set about the process of coachbuilding a rear living area using traditional methods. When the Wildgoose was first released, there were two models on offer. The Brent was one of the most ingenious designs at the time and indeed remains something of a curiosity even today. This was a body within a body, as an extending section could be raised from within the main coach-built section by means of an electric motor. It was utilizing the principle of the rising roof, but in this case it was

ABOVE: Original press release picture of the Mini Wildgoose, surely one of the strangest concepts in the UK history of motorcaravans. Take a Mini van, cut off the rear behind the cab and then build on a miniature coach-built section.

RIGHT: Did I say small door? Well, small it may be, but it was a little over-engineered – the thickness of the wood used was quite something. Every inch of space required a purpose in a camper of this size; note the storage pocket in the lower area of the door.

the remaining half of the body that was raised. Examples of the Brent model had an auxiliary method of raising the body in case of electrical failure (or flat battery), which was a cranking mechanism using a cycle chain assembly. This VEB (vertically extending body) model was dropped from the Wildgoose listing in 1966, although it is unclear if this was due to it being the most unpopular of the two models, or if it was uneconomic to produce.

The remaining model, which stayed in production throughout the life of the Wildgoose, was the Popular. Within the Popular range were two options, the Popular 2 and the Popular $3\frac{1}{2}$. These figures referred to the number of sleeping berths provided, the half representing a child. At most, the Wildgoose was no

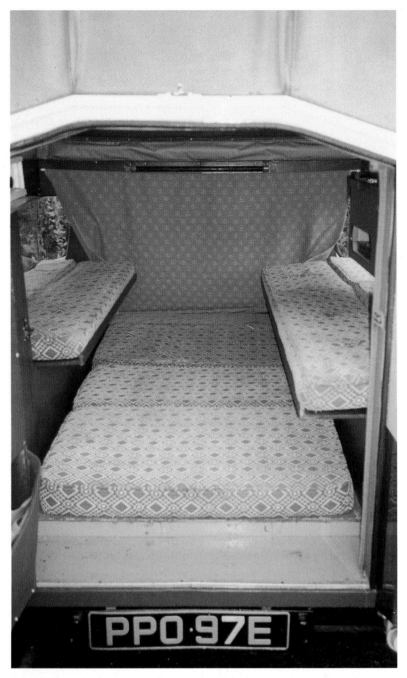

ABOVE: *This particular Wildgoose is a five-berth example. There is a double bed on the floor of the camper; the bed on the right measures 6ft × 2ft (1,829mm × 610mm) and the one on the left measures 5ft × 2ft (1,524mm × 610mm). There is also a stretcher bunk within the roof space.*

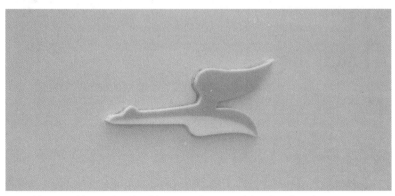

LEFT: *Wildgoose emblem on the sides of the camper. One can only imagine where the name was derived from, but many Mini enthusiasts have been on a bit of a 'Wildgoose chase' in search of surviving examples!*

more than a two-berth model and that was being optimistic – even as a two-berth, a couple of period road-test reports indicated that the occupants had to sleep 'head to tail' in order to obtain a degree of comfort at night. One also has to remember that with the coach-built body added the Mini Wildgoose became a full 2½cwt heavier than the original van, yet it was still powered by the small 848cc petrol engine.

Turning to the conversion itself, it was the traditional aluminium skin over a wooden frame. The Popular model with rising roof will be described here as this remained in production longer than the VEB option. The aluminium body was topped with a front-hinged rising roof of similar design to that found on the VW Westfalia conversion. The flexible fabric was Vynide material and incorporated two Perspex windows and a roof ventilator. With the roof in the raised position there was a full 7ft 3in (2,210mm) of headroom at the highest point. Entry into the vehicle was via a three-quarter-size single rear door. Interior furniture was constructed from plywood that had been coated with lacquer, while chrome hinges and handles were used as fittings. Entering through the rear door, there was a wardrobe to the left fitted with a single door and the two-burner hob (no grill) was situated on top of this. Opposite this was a small sink with folding drainer; neither the cooker nor sink could be used without first raising the roof. Water for the sink was stored in three 2gal (9ltr) containers that were supplied as standard. The interior sides of the vehicle were allotted to facing bench seats; the table was placed between these seats and stored neatly in the roof space when not in use.

The Wildgoose retained the factory bucket seats in the driving cab, but a single bench seat was added to carry rear passengers. Both head and legroom were somewhat restricted in this rear seat. At night these seats folded completely flat to form a double bed measuring 6ft 6in × 3ft 2in (1,981mm × 965mm). The side bench seats, which were used for dining, extended at night on metal brackets to give one single bed of 6ft by 1ft 7in (1,829mm × 483mm) and another single (a child's) of 4ft 9in × 1ft 7in (1,448mm × 483mm). Additional cushions for these single beds were housed in the cupboard.

ABOVE: *This is the curious little box mounted onto the roof of the base vehicle, the purpose of which was to house the spare wheel and tools. The lid has a front hinge and is lockable.*

RIGHT: *Internally, this was camping at its most basic. These are the cooking facilities within the camper, located in the rear corner.*

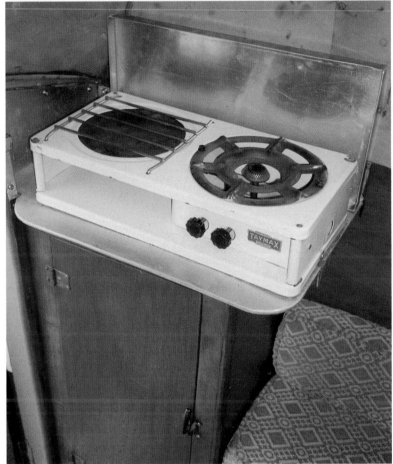

A stretcher bunk was available as an option for the roof space.

Additional storage space was provided under the rear bench seat and a generous size pocket was incorporated into the rear door. Only one light was fitted as standard within the living area and curtains were provided for all windows. The floor covering consisted of good-quality linoleum and recesses were fitted into the floor for the gas bottle and battery. A nice styling touch was the windows on each side of the rear living area. These were placed just behind the cab and were of a wraparound design, which complemented the exterior lines of the Wildgoose coachwork. Built onto the cab of the Mini was a wooden contoured box that housed the spare wheel and tool kit.

One interesting point with relation to acquiring a Wildgoose was the fact that Wildgoose Ltd was prepared to build on a van supplied by a customer. Using a price guide listing from 1967 these were the charges relating to the Wildgoose: the Popular 2 as a finished model was £867, or built on a customer's van it was £445. The Popular 3¹/₂ was £902 complete, or £480 when a customer's van was supplied. There was a very interesting addition offered by the company, and it wasn't a fridge or chemical toilet! A small, very attractive touring caravan, the Wildgoose Caravan, could be purchased to tow behind the Mini van or another vehicle. The external bodywork was of a similar styling to the Mini Wildgoose and the caravan came with the option of a fixed roof or rising roof. Wildgoose Ltd also offered the caravan as a basic shell for customers to complete and customize to their own liking.

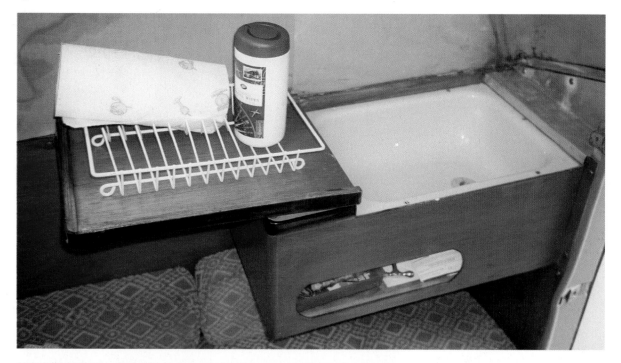

ABOVE: In the opposite corner to the cooker, the sink and draining facility.

LEFT: It is little surprise that this stunning Mini Wildgoose attracts crowds of admirers wherever it appears. It does also manage to pick up one or two trophies along the way!

A small number of the Mini Wildgoose models are still in existence around the world (eleven are known at the time of writing) and are in great demand throughout the classic Mini fraternity. Of all the (non VW-based) classic motorcaravans around today, it is probably the Mini Wildgoose that has represented the best investment. The very high prices of the remaining Wildgoose models have sent many a hopeful purchaser on a 'Wildgoose chase' in recent years!

Despite its rather small dimensions, the Goodwin family do make very good use of the Wildgoose. It is pictured here camping among the apple trees of a French orchard during an overseas rally with the Classic Camper Club.

rising-roof designs and styles

How many types of roof can you spot in this late 1960s photograph? This was the scene outside the D. Turner (Garages) Ltd site towards the end of the swinging decade. D. Turner was an agent for some of the leading conversions of the time and was a long-running and well-respected name in the world of motorcaravan sales. Models by the likes of CI/Motorized, Dormobile and Car-Campers adorn the forecourt of Derek's premises.

Although the rising, or elevating, roof had been seen firstly on the VW conversion in Germany as early as the beginning of the 1950s, it would not be until the mid-1950s that this increased style of headroom would appear on a conversion in the UK. This chapter will look at some of the popular styles from the classic period, beginning with the very first, Calthorpe.

CALTHORPE

When period motoring publications released during the middle of the 1950s made reference to Maurice Calthorpe, the originator of the rising roof, the term 'UK' should of course have been added to these statements. That first UK rising roof was no mean feat of engineering and consisted of shaped wooden sections with hand-grips in the centre. These sections were hinged on pieces of wood attached to the main metal roof. They were pushed both up and outwards against aluminium panels that covered a pre-cut hole in the van roof. When pressure was applied, the aluminium panels lifted up to form an arch in conjunction with the wooden side sections. This system was

both elaborate, yet very simple, and not only was it extremely effective but the external appearance was very pleasing. Windows were also incorporated into the wooden side sections, allowing occupants to see out and also letting more light into the living area.

As noted at the beginning of this book, Maurice Calthorpe is attributed with producing the very first post-war production coach-built model in the UK. So it seems a little strange that he should take the trouble of making a coach-built model, then adding his rising roof to it. No doubt he was equally proud of producing both the first coach-built model and the first rising roof, so he decided to combine the two! He certainly wasted no time in publicizing the fact. He immediately loaned one model to a motoring magazine so that some of its writers could carry out and publish a full account of their travels in the new Calthorpe Home Cruiser. A different vehicle (proving that he built more than one) was used to make a short news feature for *Pathe News* in 1957. This film clip involves Maurice and a colleague going for a picnic in the country with two female travellers, one of which happened to be TV, radio

and film personality Dora Bryan, together-er with her caged budgie!

Within months, the coach-built Calthorpe model had disappeared from the listings, to be replaced by a panel van conversion on the Bedford CA van. This model was still named the Home Cruiser and still featured the rising roof. As the years progressed, Maurice released further models on a variety of base vehicles, with the Calthorpe roof always fitted as standard. European Cars Ltd obviously saw the benefit of the Calthorpe roof and Maurice Calthorpe granted the company a licence to fit his roof to its VW Slumber-wagen models. Maurice Calthorpe didn't carry out conversions on the VW, but he at least had his roof attached to one of them!

DORMOBILE

Close on the heels of Calthorpe were Martin Walter Ltd (Dormobile), who produced a roof that was to become synonymous with Dormobile panel van conversions. That side-hinged roof with the candy-stripe material has surely become one of the most famous roof designs ever fitted to a motorcaravan. It

OPPOSITE PAGE:

Perhaps just about the most famous roof of the classic period, the side-hinged rising roof by Dormobile.

THIS PAGE:

Similar in style to the early Westfalia roofs, this is the front-hinged rising roof as fitted to the early Car-Camper models.

was first seen on the Dormobile Caravan based on the Bedford CA, although this was a roof of much smaller dimensions to the later model.

The Dormobile roof utilized a system of metal hoops, over which a waterproof vinyl was fixed, and worked on a concertina principle. The main roof capping was constructed from GRP and incorporated ventilators/windows into it. The huge roof did, of course, give ample room for people sleeping in this area on stretcher bunks. Earlier versions of the Dormobile roof gained quite a lot of criticism from road testers because of the amount of condensation found to be dripping from inside the roof when it

was in the raised position. This problem was overcome on later versions when a lining was added; this not only eliminated the condensation problem, but also made it much warmer.

In 1970 the *Daily Telegraph* ran a competition for the best design involving a motorcaravan. Joint winners had come up with the same idea of a Dormobile roof that opened right through 180 degrees. The design was actually constructed by Dormobile and fitted to a Bedford CF Romany model. It was a clever design and very well executed by the Dormobile staff. The GRP roof capping hinged right over the side of the vehicle and, with the support of

steel poles, actually formed an awning/ sun canopy on the side. The press, who were present at the unveiling, were very enthusiastic about the winning design, but Dormobile treated it as more of a design exercise than a real development opportunity. The Bedford was used as an exhibit, being shown at the Wilsons Motor Caravan Centres and various outdoor shows.

CAR-CAMPER

Auto Conversions began conversions on the Austin 152 in 1958; the model was given the name Car-Camper. This panel van conversion used a roof that

A pair of Bedford CA campers: left is the Romany by Dormobile; right the Calthorpe Home Cruiser. Certainly two easily identifiable roof types from days gone by.

OPPOSITE PAGE:

TOP: CI/Motorized designed and built its in-house rising roof. The Parkestone model was fitted to the Bedford Brigand, Commer Wanderer and Transit Wayfarer. A very simple system was employed to simply push the whole assembly up from inside the camper. This was a solid-sided design and incorporated windows to each side section. A Commer Wanderer example is seen here.

MIDDLE: Had there been prizes for the tallest rising roof then Torcars would have surely been in the running. This is the rising roof attached to its BMC van conversion, the Sun-Tor. As owners of such models will testify, the sides and ends are actually see-through in the evenings when the lights are on, whoops!

BOTTOM: The Airborne roof was one of the most attractive styles of the 1960s. Solid-sided with large side windows, the Airborne models never did enjoy the popularity that they deserved. Seen here is the Thames model, with some minor modifications.

THIS PAGE:

ABOVE: If the Torcars roof can be classed as one of the tallest roofs, then this Spacemaker roof is certainly the most spacious of all rising-roof options. These roofs were absolutely huge inside and could sleep an army of people! The Spacemaker roof was fitted to nearly all the popular base vehicles including Commer, Sherpa and Volkswagen. It is captured here based on the Toyota Rio.

BELOW: Gareth Haylett worked for several motorcaravan concerns over the years including Devon and Torcars. In the mid-1970s he began his own conversion business and produced some really fine examples, mostly on the Commer base and given the name Haylett Olympian. The roof design was simple, neat and effective, consisting of a GRP roof capping with fabric sides and ends, and incorporating clear plastic windows.

was similar in style to the front-hinged Westfalia design. A GRP roof capping of fairly thin proportions was hinged at the front of the metal van roof. But whereas the Westfalia-style roof was of a one-piece fabric design, the fabric on the Car-Camper roof had a seam that allowed it to fold in on itself when it was lowered. The GRP roof capping had no colouring agent added to it, so it therefore remained translucent, allowing extra light into the living area. An amber roof ventilator was fitted in the centre of the roof capping. The company continued using this type of roof design into the early 1960s, before eventually switching to the Sherwood rising roof.

WEATHERSHIELDS

The Weathershields rising roof first came into prominence when fitted to Commer's own conversion in 1960. This roof had a low-profile GRP roof cap with a centre ventilator fitted and was of the concertina type. The concertina material was a nylon-reinforced PVC, the pleated joints allowing it to fold up and down very easily. Clear PVC panels were built into the roof lining for both viewing purposes and to let more light into the vehicle. The whole system was operated via a metal frame, utilizing a spring action; it was therefore self-supporting when in the raised position.

Some degree of care had to be exercised, however, when lowering the roof, as fingers could become trapped if not placed correctly (I can vouch for this personally!).

The roof was very popular as a fitting for DIY conversions throughout the 1960s and was also used extensively on Richard Holdsworth panel van conversions. VW camper enthusiasts will readily identify this roof, as it was fitted to many Devon conversions during the 1970s.

AUTO-SLEEPER

The first Auto-Sleeper model appeared in 1961, a panel van conversion of the BMC J2. It featured a rising-roof design that would really stand the test of time, as it is still fitted to the company's VW model more than forty years later. This was, and indeed still is, a roof with solid sides and end panels; it is operated on a hinged and track system. This roof was pushed both upwards and forwards via hinged front and rear sections. This was achieved by means of a spring mechanism. The solid side panels were then pushed up and into position, being secured to the front and rear sections by slide bolts.

The side sections of the roof featured windows and these side sections were capable of being left locked in a slightly open position in order to ease ventilation during hot spells. The GRP roof capping, which was slightly bevelled around the edges, had an opening roof ventilator fitted as standard. The whole interior of this roof was fully insulated and curtains were fitted to the side windows.

The original roof, as fitted to the 1961 BMC J2, was far more of a basic box design and a forerunner of the later type as fitted to such models as the Commer Auto-Sleeper, Bedford CF, Ford Transit, Leyland Sherpa and VW.

ABOVE: The unmistakable lines of the solid-sided design by Auto-Sleepers, a great piece of engineering that has stood the test of time. First seen on top of the company's BMC J2 conversion in 1960, it is still in production today and offered as an option on the VW model. It is pictured here mated to the Bedford CF.

RIGHT: The Auto-Sleeper roof once more, but this time in the lowered position and viewed from the floor of the camper.

The Auto-Sleeper roof was perfected over many years and fitted to a variety of base vehicles, which included the Commer, Bedford CF, Transit and Sherpa, Renault Trafic and Talbot Express. Seen here on the VW Type 25 Auto-Sleeper VT20.

PARKSTONE

This rising roof was designed by CI Auto-homes and was fitted to its trio of panel van conversions, the Brigand, Wanderer and Wayfarer. The basic principle for this roof was similar to the Auto-Sleeper example, as the Parkstone was also solid-sided. But whereas the sides of the Auto-Sleeper design were upright, these were angled. When in the upright position the appearance was more akin to a tent without the point, rather than the more angular lines on similar designs.

The Parkstone had two oblong windows in each side and these remained visible on the roof, even when the roof was closed. Sliding bolts held both the front and end panels in position when raised. Curtains were fitted as standard, and two stretcher bunks could be housed to accommodate children.

CANTERBURY PITT, KENEX, TORCARS, GENTLUX

These particular roof names have been combined in one section because they all worked on a very similar principle. The roof used by Canterbury-Pitt on such base vehicles as the Ford Thames and Volkswagen was first introduced in

the early 1960s and was of the vertically extending variety. A strong waterproof vinyl was fixed to a metal framework. The roof capping was of GRP material with a built-in ventilator. One slight deviation from this design came with the introduction of the Sunshine roof, a roof with opening side panels for extra ventilation during the summer. It was never a great sales success and was dropped from the Canterbury-Pitt options soon after. When Canterbury-Pitt became Canterbury Industrial Products Ltd, use of the traditional vertically extending roof continued on the highly successful Ford Transit Canterbury.

Kenex was another converter that preferred the vertically extending type of rising roof. Again, this was a metal frame to which a vinyl material was fixed and the usual GRP roof capping was added with a ventilator. However, Kenex fitted both large and small versions of this roof to its model range. The smaller roof type was quite wide, filling the width of the vehicle, but the length finished some way short of the metal roof over the driving cab. The larger variation was extremely big and in fact covered the whole of the vehicle roof. This larger roof was first seen on the Standard Atlas Kenex Carefree model.

The first model from Torcars in 1968 saw the company making use once more of the vertically extending type of rising roof, but this time with much more added height due to the small size of the Austin A55 base vehicle. Indeed, the roof looked rather out of proportion to the conversion, but this was absolutely necessary in order to give full standing height for the occupants. Torcars always used a completely white vinyl for the roof, in contrast to most other converters who tended to use a candy-stripe effect of either red and white, or blue and white.

Throughout the 1960s advertisements would appear in the motoring press offering a rising-roof kit for DIY enthusiasts. This Gentlux roof, as with others in this section, employed the vertical approach, with vinyl fixed once again to a metal frame and a GRP roof capping. The vinyl material used by Gentlux was often red and white in colour with very wide horizontal bands of contrasting colours around it.

SHERWOOD

The Sherwood rising roof was a solid-sided example. It was the standard fitment to the later Car-Camper conversions on the Commer and Ford Transit. Although this roof had solid side and end panels, they were not constructed using wood, but with GRP. The roof operated via a series of long piano hinges and sliders, with the sides and end panels all lying flat when closed within the GRP roof capping. During the 1960s the GRP roof panels were not painted and remained translucent, but in the 1970s they were painted white. This roof also appeared on the Inca models based on the Bedford CF and Transit during the 1970s.

A roof of a very similar style to the Sherwood was used on the Airborne conversions during the 1960s and was fitted to such models as the Ford Thames and Transit.

SPACEMAKER

This was a huge canvas roof fitted to models released during the 1970s, most notably the models in the line-ups of Motorcaravan Conversions Ltd, Motorhomes International and Viking Motorhomes Ltd. The Spacemaker was a side-hinged roof, of a similar style to the famous Dormobile roof. But whereas the Dormobile example had the

material side coming down level with the edge of the vehicle, the Spacemaker roof protruded slightly beyond the width of the vehicle.

This was a roof of enormous proportions, designed to sleep three people. The vast majority of rising roofs around during the classic period were of a vinyl material, but the Spacemaker was actually canvas and had two large clear plastic windows in the side. Because this roof

used such a large amount of canvas, it required quite a deep GRP roof capping – as a result, in the closed position the roof could sometimes look to be at odds with the vehicle and certainly was not the most streamlined finish of a rising-roof model. Just some of the factory conversions fitted with the Spacemaker roof were Fiat Amigo, Toyota Rio Grande, VW Viking and the Buccaneers (available on several chassis).

Land Rover 4 × 4 models were not exempt from conversion to camper and seen here is the Park Ranger model by Motor Caravan Conversions. Pictured at the COLEX show of 1969, this conversion had a huge lift-out roof with side windows, ideal for viewing those wild animals whilst on safari!

A nicely styled high top in GRP: proof that not all GRP high-top offerings have to resemble an upturned bath. This model was rare when new and is even more so now; this is the Commer Ebor by York.

ABOVE: Almost a carbon copy of the Paralanian, with the exception of this lovely detail over the rear door. This is the Tourstar based on the Commer.

LEFT: Delightful period styling at its best, the Paralanian. The main idea of any well-designed roof must be to get water to run off as quickly as possible, a brief Central Garage certainly stuck to on the MK III Paralanian. Pictured here is a one-off custom-build on the Austin 152; this one had a side entry door.

BELOW LEFT: The Sherwood roof on this Car-Camper Transit was constructed entirely of GRP and wood. The roof employed a system of runners and hinges to operate.

During the 1960s and 1970s several of the roof designs mentioned here were actually available for DIY fitting (with the exception of Auto-Sleeper). Surprisingly, even Dormobile issued press releases to the effect that it was prepared to fit one of its roofs to a customer's own van. The motoring and motorcaravanning press carried quite literally dozens of advertisements from companies trying to sell their particular roof design to the DIY customers. As the GRP high-top styles became more popular during the 1970s, several companies began to offer a same-day fitting service on customers' own vehicles. It is worth reflecting on the fact that the high-top roof did actually replace the rising-roof in the popularity stakes as the years passed by.

weird and wonderful camper designs

A rather wonderful ex-German postal van. It must have been crying out to be converted into a camper, nicely finished in a period colour scheme.

As you might expect, not every motor-caravan produced since the middle of the 1950s was a hit with the buyers. There were certainly some weird, wonderful and altogether strange models released. This chapter will take a look some of these conversions, not all of which were complete failures by any means.

MINI CAMPERS

Some of the more outrageous campers were based on the BMC Mini. While the Wildgoose model was certainly one of the better attempts at converting the popular little runabout, there were others. One of these appeared in 1964 and was based on the Mini pick-up. The Murray Pick-a-back was a demountable living box designed to fit onto the bed of a Mini pick-up. Supporting metal legs were lowered into position on the

ground, then the living unit was raised slightly, allowing the Mini to be driven away. When this model was released in 1964, the living unit was priced at £190. Despite being far too large for the Mini pick-up, both in width and length, it did manage to survive as it appeared in the motoring press again two years later, unless of course that was simply a last-ditch effort to sell it!

Hot on the heels of the demountable offering was the Fairthorpe Caravilla, a high-top conversion on the Mini van. It is very difficult to know exactly how to describe this conversion, so I will use a quote from a road tester of the time: 'With all due respect to the designer, the external appearance is somewhat of a mobile coffin'. The rear of the Mini had been extended in order to provide interior wardrobes and standing height. The factory roof of the van had been removed and a huge box was then fitted

to the outer edges – the road tester mentioned above really best summed up the resulting appearance! The converters were hoping that the Caravilla would be marketed through BMC dealers; most likely it never was. The price of this model in 1964 was £668.

Staying with the Mini, I came across design plans for a very cute little conversion based on the Mini Countryman; this conversion was called 'Bumble'. I'm a little uncertain if this conversion was ever marketed but the plans were certainly published in a motorcaravan magazine. If it wasn't released, then a good design may have slipped through the net, as it was certainly one of the most common-sense conversions ever planned for the Mini. The designer was a marine engineer who proposed cutting away the rear of the Mini at waist height behind the cab. A body would then be built using resin-bonded waterproof plywood, the overall appearance being quite attractive. A rear bench seat formed a double bed in conjunction with the two cab seats. Charles Greene of Suffolk offered to send readers a leaflet explaining in detail his design idea. One can only assume that he only ever constructed one model for his own use, which was a great pity as it was the best of the bunch.

The final Mini-based camper was possibly the most outrageous of them all, as it tried to be two different types of leisure vehicle in one. The Caraboot was quite extraordinary to say the least

Was ever a more weird camper constructed? The Euxton Caraboot was a combination of Mini van, trailer caravan and boat. Unsurprisingly, it failed to capture the public's imagination. Only one example is known in the UK and that requires complete restoration.

If this looks more like a caravan than a camper, it's because the company responsible was Dandy Caravans, more accustomed to producing touring caravans. This model was the Commer Dandy.

I would defy any knowledgeable motoring historian to identify this conversion. Believe it or not, Dormobile carried out the strange conversion in the 1960s as a custom-build job for a client. The base vehicle is the big Commer Walk-thru.

– it looked like a Mini van had reversed into a trailer caravan, which in fact it had! Built by Euxton Coachcraft Ltd of Chorley, Lancashire, the Caraboot was an incredible feat of motorcaravan design and engineering. It utilized the Mini van or Countryman, onto which a GRP rectangular box had been clipped to the roof. A GRP sailing boat was then placed upside-down on top of this box.

The converters then fitted mouldings low down along each side of the vehicle, rearward of the cab.

As you would quite rightly assume, those modifications do not make a camper and the best was yet to come. Euxton Coachcraft constructed a living module, with one set of wheels, that would slide onto the back of the Mini, utilizing the lower mouldings on the

Mini. This living module was open-ended and therefore had a cut-out that fitted over not only the Mini, but also the rectangular box and boat mounted on the roof. This meant that when the set-up was in travelling mode, it did become a six-wheeled vehicle. The rear living module had a side entrance door, side windows and one large rear window. When on site, this living module was slid

Fans of the evergreen Morris Minor may well have seen this wonderful creation around the rally scene. This home conversion was built using caravan materials and the builder did a fine job. It sleeps two adults and a child.

back on runners towards the rear of the van; this in effect created a whole living space, still attached to the Mini. Even more ingenious was the fact that the double bed was the space under the boat! Both the rectangular box and the boat could be unclipped from the top of the Mini and the rear living module pushed off the Mini completely. In free-standing mode the rear module had support jacks fitted to stabilize it and a vinyl cover to enclose the open end (which was normally slid over the Mini). The rear module was completely fitted out as a camper with dining table, seats, storage cupboards and small kitchen.

Despite being an outrageous creation, one has to hand it to the design team, for the Caraboot was certainly one of the most incredible campers ever released. Although no production records remain, the Caraboot was in production for several years, or at least made available for several years. So one has to assume that at least a small number were sold. It is known that there is at least one incomplete survivor in the UK. In the summer of 1964 the Caraboot price was £460 plus the price of a Mini van. The Caraboot could also be fitted to a customer's own Mini.

The Caraboot was not the first camper to add a boat as standard equipment; a roof boat was fitted to the Ford Thames Airborne conversion in the early 1960s.

As with the Caraboot, this was again a white GRP sailing boat fixed upside-down on the roof and clipped in position. When the boat was in use, a canvas/vinyl cover was placed over the hole/space left in the roof. Unsurprisingly, it didn't take the market by storm.

MICRO-CAMPERS

When it comes to weird and wonderful campers, those in the 'micro-section' probably have a foot in both camps, being rather weird but certainly wonderful compact designs. The campers in this section were slightly larger than the Mini-based examples, with the majority based on popular car-derived vans. Certainly one of the most popular models of this type was Torcars' Sun-Tor, which was covered in a previous chapter, but there were several others. The first of the car-derived vans to be converted to a small camper was the Roma by Dormobile, first introduced in 1967. The Roma was a conversion of the popular Bedford HA 8cwt van. This model was given the full Dormobile design treatment and was fitted with a smaller version of the famous side-hinged roof. In order to make better use of internal space Dormobile had fitted a rear canopy to the single tailgate, to give a greater amount of room for a double bed. As one might expect in

such a small van, the interior fitments were all in miniature, including the sink and cooker. The Roma two- and three-berth models were quite successful, until Dormobile released another small camper, this time based on the Ford Escort van.

In 1969 Dormobile set about converting the Escort 8cwt van. The Dormobile Elba was similar in its internal layout to the Roma. It was fitted with the Dormobile roof, small cooker and sink, and like the Roma it featured an extension at the rear in order to give extra room for sleeping. Certainly in the classification 'weird and wonderful' was the highly modified Elba GT. At the request of Wilsons Motor Caravan Centre, John Willment Ltd took a standard Elba model and set about getting a little more speed out of it. In standard form, the Elba was available with an 1100cc or 1300cc petrol engine; this particular model, designated the Elba GT, was given the engine from a 1600 GT Cortina car. In road tests it was very quick indeed, with a reported top speed in excess of 100mph.

Other models available on the Escort van during the late 1960s were the Freedom Camper, which featured a front-hinged rising roof, and a conversion by Car-Campers, better known for its conversions on the Commer and Transit. However, it was to be both the Elba by Dormobile and the Siesta by Canterbury that were among the top-selling small campers of the era. Both utilized the Escort van. Joining their ranks during the 1970s was C&W Conversions of Torrington. This new company produced a superb conversion of the MK II Escort van called the Nimbus. The address may sound familiar and that is because they were two gentlemen who left Torcars (producer of the Sun-Tor models) to start their own business. The Nimbus gained excellent reviews from the motoring press for the quality of the interior conversion, which rather unsurprisingly was very similar in style and design to the Sun-Tor.

Next in the micro-camper section comes the little Fiat 850T. Motor Caravan Conversions of Berkhamstead was responsible for producing conversions on the tiny Fiat van. Several different configurations were on offer, with or without a rising roof, but the two most popular models were the Fargo and the Fiesta.

Small micro-campers are often intriguing; this conversion by Dormobile must have exercised the skills of the company's designers. Based on the Bedford HA van, this is the Roma, a compact camper with extending rear pram-type hood and the famous roof.

Little is known about this strange coach-built model, except that it was based on the BMC J2 and given the name 'Madisons Special'.
It is almost attractive in a way, although the shape of the over-cab area never did catch on!

Another model in the micro-camper category and quite successful for Dormobile. This is the Ford Escort Elba.

Not to be outdone in this class was Dormobile, which also released a model based on the little Fiat van that included the side-hinged roof. But by far the most successful conversion on the small Fiat was the hugely popular Amigo by Motor Caravan Conversions, an updated version of its previous model, the Fiesta, by now built on the Fiat 900T. In fact, by the late 1970s the Fiat Amigo was not only the best-selling model in its class, it was one of the best-selling motorcaravans in the UK. This was due no doubt to it being extremely economical, able to fit into the average family garage and possessing a high level of standard features. The Amigo was also fitted with the huge Spacemaker roof, making it very spacious inside, despite the small floorpan.

One type of motorcaravan never quite as popular in the UK as it was/is in the USA was the demountable, or dismountable, unit. Should these necessarily be in the 'weird and wonderful' category? It could be argued that the whole concept of a demountable unit is a little strange and some of the models over the years have been fitted with living modules that were completely disproportionate in comparison with their base vehicle. Dedicated enthusiasts of this type of camper would of course argue that they have a wonderful dual-purpose role, allowing the living unit to be dropped off and the base vehicle used independently. In the UK, this type of camper really didn't enjoy any degree of success until the 1970s.

The Suntrekker models, built by B. Walker & Son Ltd of Watford, certainly helped to put the demountable models firmly on the map during the mid-1970s. These units were created for a large variety of base vehicles that included the Bedford CF 250, Datsun 300, Ford Transit, Leyland Sherpa, Land Rover, Marina, Toyota and VW LT. One of the most popular models was the Marina Suntrekker. The main problem with this type of unit, however, was that the base vehicle could be used independently of the living unit, which meant that the base vehicles came in for far more abuse through wear than a conventional motorcaravan. Often this resulted in the living unit surviving the base vehicle. Although other companies did build demountable units during the classic years, the Suntrekker models were by far the most popular. Dandy Caravans of Wigan made one very rare demountable unit, constructed on the Moskvitch 434 pick-up.

There were several campers that fell into an unclassified category, the Mini Caraboot being a case in point. The little Romahome that was based on the Honda TN7 pick-up was another such example. It was a demountable that wasn't really a demountable! The Romahome was a small GRP body attached

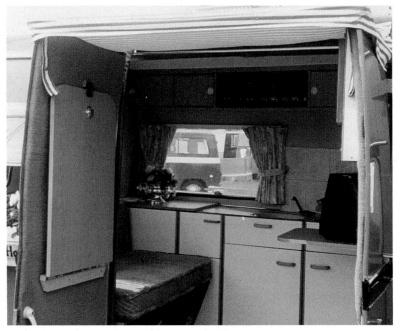

Wonderful DIY interior of the splitty postal van (see p.163). The owner did a fabulous job in this high-top VW, creating a very warm and welcoming interior.

This has to fall into both the weird and the wonderful category: the Ford Transit Canterbury Sunhome of the 1970s. It was aimed at being a cross between a coach-build and a panel van conversion. These 'turtle top' campers enjoyed greater success in the USA than in the UK, but both this model and the similar Holdsworth Hi-Flyer sold in reasonable numbers.

to the Honda pick-up chassis cab, but wasn't a demountable in the traditional sense. This was not a camper that could be used independently of the chassis when on a campsite, but the GRP living module could be detached at home in order to use the Honda chassis cab independently. The Romahome was a very successful camper and still has a big following to this day.

Motorcaravan bodies constructed using GRP were commonplace in the UK after the launch of the Dormobile Debonair on the Bedford CA. Dormobile continued this trend with its Debonair MK II on the Bedford CF and later the Land Cruiser, again on the CF. During the latter part of the 1970s a further two weird campers appeared on the market, both featuring heavy use of GRP bodywork. The Tandy Fox was a model based on the four-wheeled Reliant car, which itself was GRP to begin with. This therefore became a complete camper built using GRP for the vehicle body and the living unit.

But when it comes to weird and wonderful campers the Starcraft probably wins hands down. This was a kit-camper, very futuristic in design and again built from GRP. The name was very appropriate for this model because it really did look something akin to a UFO! Despite the 'alternative' styling used by its designers, it did in fact become quite popular with buyers who wanted something a little different. The Starcraft was designed to make use of the mechanical components from a Ford Cortina car; an extra, non-driven rear axle was also added, making it a six-wheeler.

RIGHT: A home-converted coach-build dating from the 1960s. Built from old bus and coach spares, it is very angular in appearance. It is apparently located in Scotland and was based on a BMC J2.

BELOW: It was too difficult to resist including these brightly coloured ERF Roadrangers in the wonderful category. Back in the classic period, converters were not afraid to use garish colours to catch the eye. But I really don't believe that these colours were ever an option offered by the Jennings company!

ABOVE: Weird designs were not confined to the UK scene, although the styling on the German Mercedes Orion model is rather appealing.

LEFT: The Buddicum sisters of Sussex were well known for their choice of custom-built campers during the 1960s. It was they who had the Paralanian with the side entry door built to order. This was their final creation, the Commer Aardvark, designed by them and built at Barking Garage. It had a fascinating interior designed around their beloved pet cats (who travelled with them). The sisters have now passed on, but thankfully an enthusiast rescued the camper and is currently restoring it.

My final two candidates in the weird classification were models released during the 1970s. The term 'turtle top' originated from the USA and was used to describe a camper (panel van conversion) that had a high top fitted, the front section of which overhung the driving cab, thus creating the turtle-top appearance. This style of GRP high top never did find favour with UK buyers, but it didn't stop two renowned companies from attempting to popularize the style. Richard Holdsworth released the Holdsworth Hi-Flyer based on the Ford Transit, while Canterbury released the Canterbury Sunhome. They were both very similar in external appearance and the increased headroom and internal space created the illusion that one was in a coach-build rather than a panel van. Both models met with a modicum of success, although strong crosswinds on a motorway or open road provided a very interesting experience!

a calendar of motorcaravan facts and figures

Wilsons Motor Caravan Centre in London probably sold more motorcaravans during the 1950s, '60s and '70s than any other dealer in the UK. In fact, many people regarded Leslie Wilson as 'Mr Motorcaravan'. The Wilson family did a great deal to promote the new leisure activity in its infancy. Pictured here is the Wilsons' own conversion, the Adventurer, based on the large Commer.

This final chapter provides a summary of the most notable points of interest from the classic years. It takes the form of an easy-to-follow calendar and should prove to be a useful reference tool for all motoring historians and classic camper enthusiasts.

1956

■ Peter Pitt releases the first fully fitted camper on the UK market (post-war).

1957

■ Maurice Calthorpe is credited with being the innovator of the rising roof in the UK. He also releases the first production coach-built model this year based on the Bedford CA.

Maurice also features in a *Pathe News* item showing off the new model; the news clip features personality Dora Bryan and friends going for a picnic in the Calthorpe. Martin Walter Ltd (Dormobile) releases its Dormobile Caravan featuring a side-hinged rising roof; this version was much smaller in comparison with the later roof.

■ Central Garage of Bradford unveils the Paralanian coach-build, a luxury two-berth model based on the BMC J2.

■ Lisburne Garage Ltd of Torquay (VW dealer) collaborates with cabinetmaker Jack P. White of Sidmouth to produce a VW camper.

■ Taylor Motor Body Conversions of Norfolk announces its new model, the Bedmobile, based on the

Bedford CA. Eight different variations are available, including the cheapest model on the market, the Standard Special; it carried a price tag of just £585.

1958

■ Auto-Conversions commenced production of its Car-Camper models on the BMC J2 chassis.

■ Bluebird introduced its coach-built Highwayman model, also using the BMC J2 (Austin and Morris variants).

■ Wessex Motors Ltd of Salisbury announced a conversion on the J2 to be called the Wessex Car-O-Van.

■ Moortown Caravan Conversions of Leeds released its panel van model based on the VW Microbus, the Moortown Autohome.

1959

- Reports in *Autocar* this year indicated that Martin Walter Ltd was now building as many as eighty Dormobile Caravans per week. Even this rate of production was far below demand for the vehicle and so the factory premises were extended in order to cope with increasing sales.
- Lisburne Garage Ltd was one of the first converters to take out a full-page advertisement in a monthly motoring publication. The advertisement featured the company's very successful Devon Caravette based on the VW.
- By the end of the year there were thirteen coachbuilders offering motorcaravans, with Martin Walter Ltd having the biggest share of this new market.

1960

- By midway through this year that list of thirteen coachbuilders had rapidly increased to seventeen, ten of them taking stand space at the Earls Court Motor Show. At this show, Martin Walter Ltd announced its improved rising roof, Peter Pitt also revealed his Sunshine roof with opening panels.
- Lisburne announced improvements to its Austin Sleep-A-Car, in the process reducing the price by £85.
- There was now so much interest in this new leisure activity that a specialist owners club was formed to cater for them, the Motorcaravanners Club.
- To coincide with the release of the Commer 1500 van, Commer announced its in-house conversion, the Commer Caravan.
- The first coach-build on the new Rootes Commer was also announced, the luxury Hadrian.
- Another new van release this year was the BMC J4, which was quickly given the Dormobile treatment by Martin Walter Ltd.
- The most expensive model on the market remained the Land Cruiser by Land Cruisers Ltd of London; this was priced at £1,500 and built on the big 30cwt Commer. The industry reported that the total number of motorcaravans sold in 1960 was 900.

1961

- Auto-Sleepers Ltd of Wood Stanway, Gloucestershire, entered the motorcaravan market with a panel van conversion of the BMC J2.
- Market leaders, Martin Walter Ltd, decided to drop conversions on the BMC J2 and also announced a conversion on the VW Kombi, to be called the Flair.
- Central Garage of Bradford released the MK III Paralanian, now with a restyled exterior. As a road test and PR exercise, editorial staff of *Motor* magazine took a Paralanian across to France for use as both sleeping accommodation and an office during the Le Mans race in June.
- The Dover-based coachbuilders Kenex added GRP tail fins to its Bedford CA conversion, very similar to those on the Bedford Dormobile.
- The Bluebird Highwayman continued to be the best-selling coach-built example on offer, with some restyling this year. The company also announced that its panel van conversion, the Moto-Plus, was enjoying good sales.
- Peter Pitt entered into an agreement with Canterbury Industrial Products Ltd (initially named Canterbury Sidecars Ltd) that allowed the company to produce his designs under licence.
- Despite the A- and B-Series models failing to achieve good sales figures, the Kingscote and Stephens luxury C-Series Cotswold coach-build gained many admirers.
- Martin Walter Ltd was the first to offer a 4 × 4 option with a conversion of the Land Rover and in true off-road styling it was fitted with stove-enamelled metal cabinetwork.
- In April of this year Commer attempted to break into the American market by displaying its Commer Caravan at the New York Motor Show.

1962

- Martin Walter Ltd now offered six different base vehicles, with twenty-eight variations upon them.
- One of the most interesting new models for this year made its debut, the Space Traveller by Locomotors Ltd of Macclesfield. This was an intriguing coach-build with quite futuristic styling, available on either the BMC J2 or Commer.
- Not unlike the Space Traveller was the Sunquest by Thomas Hosking and Son Ltd of Cardiff. This featured a one-piece GRP roof and single rear-door entry. The Sunquest was only available on the BMC J2.
- Another 4 × 4 vehicle now on offer was the Carawagon by R. J. Searle Ltd of Middlesex. This model retailed at £1,180, in comparison with the Land Rover Dormobile at £1,198.
- The only UK company to offer a conversion on the little Renault Estafette was Coachwork Conversions Ltd of Berkhamstead. Its delightful Touriste model was designed to sleep two adults and one child. It didn't make use of a rising roof, staying instead with the fixed metal factory roof. This was a four-door model incorporating a side-entry door.
- Other conversions now on the market included the VW Service by Service Garages, the M.T.S. Buccaneer by M.T.S., and based on the Bedford CA, BMC J2, Commer, Ford Thames or Standard Atlas, and the final newcomer, the Highlander by Ryan Motorized Caravans of Worthing. This was available on either the Bedford CA or BMC J4.
- New this year was the Caraversions model on the VW Kombi. This London-based company offered a very unusual high-top design, which looked a little out of sorts. The high top was a bit large in relation to the base vehicle; it wasn't a firm favourite with buyers.

1963

- This year saw the disappearance of some well-known names from the listings; these included Calthorpe, Wessex, M.T.S., Nomad and Kenex of Dover. Kenex, makers of the Carefree range, was taken over by Martin Walter Ltd, although utility vans and vehicles continued to be built under the Kenex brand.
- Once again, motorcaravans featured well at the Earls Court Motor Show.

Martin Walter Ltd showed its Bedford Deauville, Bedford Romany, Ford Thames, Land Rover and VW models. Central Garage of Bradford not only had its luxury Paralanian coach-build, but also a more economical panel van conversion, the Paravan. This made use of the metal factory roof of a BMC J2 and was sold as a utility vehicle. The interior was removable, allowing the owner to use the vehicle as a van if required. The Paravan was also available in kit form for DIY fixing. Other models on display included the Devon VW range, the Cotswold range, Hadrian coach-built examples and, finally, the Bluebird Highwayman. Bluebird had recently reached an agreement to sell the Highwayman model in the USA, although for the American market it would be renamed the Sunbeam Funwagon.

- Jack P. White of Sidmouth, responsible for the wooden interiors of all Devon conversions, passed away this year.

1964

- This was a year of consolidation within the motorcaravan industry, with fewer new models released. One vehicle entering its first full year of hopeful sales was the Adventurer. This was a large luxury coach-built model on offer by Wilsons Motor Caravan Centre in London. It was based on the big 30cwt Commer with the 2965cc petrol engine, and at £2,500 it was easily the most expensive model of the time.
- Another new name appearing this year was that of Auto-Homes, with its Adventuress model. This was a panel van conversion of the Ford Thames 10–15cwt vans; a rising roof was an extra £70.
- As for the rest of the converters, it was really a status quo affair with things remaining pretty much as in the previous year. This would be the last full year of production for the Ford Thames van (10–15cwt) and also for the Commer 1500, which would be revised the following year.

- For the first time, road casualty figures begin to make real headlines. Figures published in the motoring press indicated that 385,499 people were either killed or injured on UK roads. The number of deaths in road traffic accidents was 7,820, an increase of 13 per cent on the previous year.

1965

- This was a very busy year in the annals of UK motorcaravan history. One vehicle introduced this year would not only have an immediate impact upon motorcaravanning, but would also change the face of light commercial vans in the UK forever, the Ford Transit. Within months of it being released, three conversions appeared on the motorcaravan listings, Car-Camper, Coachwork Conversions Freedom and Dormobile.
- Another change this year, relating to base vehicles, featured the Commer. The body shape remained exactly

When Ford released the Transit in 1965 one of the first conversions to appear was this Freedom model by Coachwork Conversions. They had previously enjoyed only minimal success with its Renault Estafette Touriste model.

the same, but was improved both mechanically (upgraded to a 1725cc engine) and cosmetically. It was now given the designation of the Commer PA.

- One established model to disappear this year was the Hadrian coach-build. Quick to fill the void, however, was J. H. Jennings of Sandbach with its Roadranger models. With the interior design almost identical to the Paralanian (same designer), the first models were built on the BMC J2 and Commer.

- One model given a name change this year was the Murray Pickaback based on the Mini; from 1965 it was to be called simply Pickaback.

- As well as the changes made to the Commer engine size and exterior trim, the popular panel van conversion, the Commer Caravan, was discontinued in order that Chrysler could focus its attentions on supplying chassis to Bluebird for the Commer Highwayman. The Highwayman (Sunbeam Funwagon in America) was displayed at the Californian Sportsman's Show; orders worth around £2,800,000 were received. The Commer was enjoying buoyant times, as Auto-Sleepers Ltd had now dropped the use of the BMC J2 in favour of the Commer-only option.

- The new GRP-bodied Debonair (unveiled in 1964) by Martin Walter Ltd now meant that Dormobile models were selling well in both panel van and coach-built categories.

- For the serious motorcaravanner, Cotswold released its D-series model based on the BMC FG chassis. A luxury two-berth, with the option of two further berths, it was to be one of the largest models on sale in the UK; price when launched was £2,950.

1966

- This year the Bluebird range of motorcaravans was sold under the name of Caravans International (Motorized) Ltd (CI/M); the biggest-selling model remained the Commer Highwayman. The company's panel van conversion, the Wayfarer, became the Wanderer

and was now fitted with the Parkstone rising roof.

- This year also saw the introduction of the first coach-built model on the new Ford Transit. CI/M released the Transit Sprite Motorhome.

- Names to disappear this year from the listings included the Locomotors Space Traveller and the Caraversions on the VW. Another model to be dropped by the end of this year was the Touriste on the Renault Estafette, replaced by the Commer Camper Coach.

- In an attempt to build up a market on the continent, Dormobile was importing Ford Transits in left-hand-drive format from Cologne. These were being converted into Dormobile motorcaravans and then shipped back over in finished form.

- Pegasus released a slightly different conversion on the Bedford CA. The Pegasus MK III featured swivel captain's seats in the cab, an annexe built into the rear tailgate and furniture made from GRP. Wildgoose of Worthing introduced a trailer caravan this year to complement its Mini Wildgoose conversion.

- Conversions on the Volkswagen continued to sell extremely well, with Devon leading the way. A recent addition to the listings, Danbury (Multicar), was offering three VW conversions on the Transporter, Kombi and Microbus. The most expensive model available 'off the peg' remained the six-berth Adventurer by Wilsons at £3,000.

- The first specialist monthly magazine for motorcaravanners went on sale this year, the brainchild of the late John Hunt. The magazine was launched as *Motor Caravan + Camping*. It remains in circulation today as *Motorcaravan, Motorhome, Monthly (MMM)*.

1967

- One of the most notable points of interest this year was the introduction of the new Volkswagen T2 in August and, with it, the demise of the split-screen model. One newcomer to the scene was Richard Holdsworth who began his long stay within the industry by offering conversions on the new VW. The

new VW was also added to the list of Dormobile models, with Canterbury and Danbury utilizing the VWT2.

- Two completely new models for the year included the Transit Wayfarer by CI/M and the Dormobile Landcruiser based on the BMC 250JU. One new model only available to order was the Webster Bedford CA. This was a conversion of the Bedford CA panel van and featured a quality wooden interior, plus a rising roof. Although the converter, Ron Webster, didn't enjoy great sales with this model, he was to enjoy more success as the co-founder of Torcars a year later.

1968

- The luxury Paralanian model was now being produced by Spen Coachbuilders Ltd, now that Central Garage of Bradford was no longer building motorcaravans. The almost identical Tourstar model was on the market, built by European Caravans Ltd.

- Cotswold introduced a new model this year, the C-series Major. This was both longer and wider than the standard C-series example and was to be based on the BMC 250JU. Another new model for 1968 was the Carawagon Continental by Searle, on the LWB Land-Rover station wagon.

- There were two announcements from Ford UK: one was the introduction of a high-compression version of its 2ltr V4 petrol engine; the second announcement concerned the release of a new light van, the Ford Escort.

- The Commer Highwayman continued to be the best-selling coach-build in the UK, although CI/M announced very hefty price increases across its range in June. Ron Webster and Ian Hutchinson joined forces to produce the prototype Sun-Tor based on the BMC $1/2$ ton van.

1969

- By far the biggest news item of the year was the release of the CF range of vans to replace the CA, which had been in production since 1952.

When Canterbury's licence ran out to continue producing the Pitt open-plan designs, the company switched its attention to new designs.
This was probably the first successful high-top model to enter production in the UK, the Canterbury Plainsman.

Dormobile released three new models based on the new CF, before the 'official' release of the CF range!

- Dormobile began the year with a press reception held in a hotel at London Airport. This press conference was to unveil two new models, the Escort Elba and Transit Freedom, and also to reiterate that Dormobile was a registered trade name. This was obviously a precursor to a later press release in the spring, informing everyone that Martin Walter Ltd was undergoing changes. Dormobile Ltd would from then on be applicable to the manufacturing division and Martin Walter (EKV) Ltd would handle sales and distribution of Vauxhall and Bedford trucks.

- Personality Jimmy Saville purchased a custom-built motorcaravan by Devon Conversions. This was on the Mercedes 406 chassis and had such fitments as a wardrobe capable of fitting twenty suits, a sun-bathing area on the roof, a permanent double bed and a shower/bath. Cost of this luxury Mercedes was £5,250.

- At the COLEX show this year, Dormobile displayed its new Coaster model based on the Commer and the Land Rover Park Ranger made an appearance. On public display for the first time were two of the new Sun-Tor BMC models by Torcars. Both models sold within forty-eight hours of the show opening, a sign of success to come for the Torrington company. Also on display at this show were Richard Holdsworth Commer and VW examples, the Ford Escort Freedom, Tourstar and Sundowner by European Caravans and Airborne models on the Commer and Transit.

- CI/M released an interesting statistic this year, stating that customers requesting a fridge to be fitted in their new purchase had increased from only 10 per cent in 1963 to a huge 75 per cent by 1969. Another figure of interest was the number of motorcaravans sold in the UK, which had risen to over 5,000 units in 1969. Dormobile reported that its sales for the year were 1,696 units.

- One of the saddest pieces of news to emerge this year was the death of the great motorcaravan innovator, Peter Pitt.

1970

- New models this year included the Dormobile Contessa, the Brigand and Landliner by CI/M, a new Spacequest from Thomas Hosking, the Cotswold Caravelle and the Auto-Sleeper Bedford CF. J.H. Jennings of Sandbach built a one-off custom example of its Roadranger on the big Mercedes 406D chassis and also decided to offer its standard Roadranger on the Bedford CF.

- In May, Dormobile Ltd surprised many by using the medium of television to advertise its VW model.

- Wilsons Motor Caravan Centre placed a huge order for £450,000 worth of CI/M models and in addition opened a new branch in Epsom.

- As the year came to a close, the industry claimed that over 7,000 motorcaravans had been sold in 1970.

This young lady must have been a Ford employee as she appears in many publicity pictures for Ford-based campers during the 1970s, irrespective of which company produced them. She is seen here dressed in typical 1970s attire adorning the rear doorway of the Ford Transit Landliner by CI/M.

1971

- The popularity of motorcaravans continued apace this year with Wilsons placing an order for £580,000 worth of units from CI/M.
- Torcars of Torrington was also enjoying continued success, forcing a move to larger premises with its own campsite to one side. This was also the year that the company added another model to accompany its already popular BMC Sun-Tor, a panel van conversion of the Commer with Torcars' own rising roof, the Commer Sun-Tor Major.
- Another company to release models based on the Commer this year was Oxley Coachcraft, which introduced the Balmoral and Belvedere.
- New models on the Ford Transit for 1971 were the rising roof Inca and the Autohome by CI/M.
- Dormobile unveiled three new models, the Land Cruiser on the Bedford CF, the Freeway, a rising-roof model on the CF, and a conversion of the 4 × 4 Range Rover.
- The popular Searle Carawagon Land Rover had an addition this year in the shape of the Carawagon Ranger Rover.
- Jennings built yet another luxury, one-off model for a customer, this time using the big Bedford KC chassis.
- One of the most expensive (UK built) models on offer this year was the Auto-Kabins Mercedes 408 at £10,450.
- Two well-known names to disappear from the listings this year were Airborne and European Caravans.
- The BTA (British Tourist Authority) published some very interesting figures in 1971, which were taken from a survey conducted during the previous year. It was found that 6.5 per cent of all domestic households contained one or more campers/caravanners (including motorcaravanners). From this figure, it was estimated that by 1980 the figure of 6.5 would increase to 9 per cent. Of other interest in the survey was the fact that campers and caravanners spent around £100 million on holidays, £70 million of that in the UK. Towards the end of the year, the motorcaravan industry reported that expected sales for the year would be around 8,000 units.

1972

- This was to be the year when Volkswagen upset some of the UK conversion companies by withdrawing its approval. The two to suffer were Danbury and Dormobile, with only Devon remaining as the sole approved converters of the VW T2. As from this year, only the VW Devon Caravette and the German Westfalia Continental models were available in the UK. Despite this, sales of VW-based campers were soaring.

Colindale (VW) Ltd ordered a massive £980,000 worth of Caravette and Continental models for its new VW showroom, reported to be the biggest VW camper showroom in Europe. VW (GB) Ltd announced that a record 2,919 VW campers were sold in the UK in the first four months of the year.

- With Danbury switching to the conversion of the newly imported Toyota Hiace van, the two UK giants, CI/M and Dormobile, also announced conversions on the Japanese import.

- Other new models for this year were the Bedford CF Bristolian, a coach-build by Welch & Co. of Somerset, the Haylett Olympian (panel van conversion), York unveiled its luxury coach-build, the Commer York, and Associated Caravans launched its Commer conversions, the Teamster and Clearway.

- Torcars extended its factory-attached campsite to over 2 acres. The company also produced two new models: the Marina Sun-Tor and the Torcars Range Rover.

- Two former Torcars employees created C&W Conversions and moved into the old Torcars factory to produce the Nimbus model based on the Ford Escort van.

- Dormobile enjoyed sales success with its Freeway models, announcing that £373,000 worth were sold between October 1971 and January 1972. Dormobile also revealed some sad news concerning one of its most revered employees. Designer Cecil Carte passed away this year; he had joined Martin Walter Ltd in 1922, becoming Production Manager by 1946. In the 1950s he was responsible for designing the Dormatic seats. In the mid-1950s his team designed the famous side-hinged roof. His last project was the Dormobile Roma.

- Three changes were announced by vehicle suppliers: CI/M fitted the bigger 2.5ltr V6 engine into the Landliner model; Chrysler offered a high-compression option of the 1725cc engine; and the Bedford CF engines were uprated to 1759cc and 2279cc.

- By 1972 Wilsons Motor Caravan Centre had built up its motorcaravan hire business to such an extent that it by now possessed one of the largest rental fleets in Europe. Wilsons had also begun to import the American Winnebago RVs into the UK as the European distributor. A top of the range Winnebago Brave D20 carried a price tag of £4,468.

- Madisons of Southport was appointed the northern area distributors for the Jennings Roadranger models this year.

- There was a great deal being written about the impending introduction of VAT, and the motorcaravan industry was expecting to be hit quite hard by this new tax. Several advertisements appeared in the motoring press stating, 'Purchase now – VAT is coming'. There is little doubt that motorcaravan sales had soared into five figures for the very first time by the end of 1972.

1973

- The surprise new model for this year was the all-new ERF Roadranger on the Transit. It was also offered on the Bedford CF and the A-series Ford.

- Due in part to the fuel crisis, micro-campers were gaining in popularity with models on the Morris Marina, Ford Escort and Fiat all selling in relatively high numbers. Danbury, which had switched to using the Toyota, also entered the micro market with the Huntsman based on the Fiat 850T.

- Madisons of Southport opened a new centre at Clifton, near Preston, and this had over 1 acre of sales display area. Part of this area was designated to the micro-campers, with around forty always on display.

- Devon Conversions, the only UK company to win official VW approval for its conversions, was by now producing 200 Caravette models a week at its Ramsgate factory. Ramsgate was the import destination for the VW base vehicles; the company still retained its Sidmouth factory for furniture manufacture.

- Motorcaravans were very much in vogue this year, especially with celebrities: Wilsons supplied a Winnebago to the Tyrell Grand Prix Team; Jimmy Saville purchased a Transit Landliner; Radio One DJ Johnny Walker bought a Bedford CF Auto-Sleeper from Turners of London; and Dustin Hoffman used a Commer Highwayman as his base whilst making a film in Cornwall. It was also a case of 'carry on camping' when Sid James and Barbara Windsor made an appearance at the Caravan & Camping Show at Earls Court and took the opportunity to try out many of the models on display.

- The introduction of VAT this year has a marked effect on sales during the latter half of the year. This was the final year of 'boom' sales figures, and it would take the industry several decades to recover fully. Caravans International (Motorized) Ltd, known to all as CI/M, had a change of name this year. From now on it was CI Autohomes Ltd.

1974

- Leslie Wilson, regarded by many as 'Mr Motorcaravan', retired from the board of Wilsons Motor Caravan Centre. Leslie had been instrumental in the success of motorcaravanning in the UK, having opened the first motorcaravan-only sales showroom in 1958 (the family, though, had been in the motor business since 1916).

- Another name to disappear this year was that of ERF (Jennings) Roadrangers. ERF announced that it required more factory space for truck making.

- Two names from the past reappear this year, Tourstar and Sundowner, with European Caravans Ltd once more building motorcaravans; both new models were available on the Bedford CF.

- Torcars of Torrington announced that it had formed an association with W. Mumford Ltd, a West Country BL distributor. Mumford acquires a 50 per cent share in Torcars.

- There were a couple of new models released this year; one of them was aimed at being the cheapest UK coach-build. This was a very box-like model called the Commer Dandy and it was priced at £1,600 plus VAT. Two high-top models were announced on the Mercedes 206D, the Autobahn by Bariban and the Comet by Cotswold.

- When the year came to a close, the industry announced that around 15,000 motorcaravans had been sold in the UK for 1973. It was expected that this figure would rise to 22,000 in 1974, unless the introduction of VAT and the impact of fuel shortages had an effect (in fact, that 15,000 sales figure achieved in 1973 has never been repeated).

1975

- The year commenced with news of a new van release from BLMC, the Leyland Sherpa. This van would replace the J4, although the rear of the new Sherpa would be almost identical to the older J4. Auto-Sleepers was first to launch a Sherpa-based camper, with Torcars quickly following with its Brentnor model; both were rising-roof examples. For the first time in its illustrious history, Auto-Sleepers was offering conversions based on four different chassis: Bedford CF, Commer, Transit and Sherpa.
- Sales of demountable campers had been increasing steadily during the 1970s and Suntrekker launched a vigorous sales campaign this year; it also released a unit to fit the Morris Marina pick-up.
- One of the most unusual releases of this year was the Dandy Moskvitch; it was priced at £1,200 plus VAT.
- CI Autohomes released the Travelhome and unveiled this new model at the Brussels Motor Show. This was a coach-build based on the Ford Transit 130 model. Another new coach-built model making its debut was the Advantura from European Caravans Ltd. Available on both the Bedford CF and Ford Transit, the Advantura would become one of the most popular coach-built models of the period. One more new model launched was the coach-built Toyota Newlander, which was to become one of the best-selling models based on the Japanese import.
- A name from the past making a comeback this year was the Romany from Dormobile. This was pitched at the first-time buyers (according to

Dormobile) and this MK III Romany would provide basic necessities at a price of £2,656+VAT.

- It was a case of all smiles at VW (GB) this year when the company landed a deal for £250,000 worth of Devon campers (in LHD form) for the French market. This order amounted to around 350 models, with the possibility of further orders to follow.
- However, it wasn't smiles all across the industry, as the introduction of VAT and the general economic mood meant a decline in motorcaravan sales. CI Autohomes was the first to admit that there was a decline in its sales figures, leading to the loss of around 200 jobs at the company.

Another company experiencing difficulties was Haylett Motorcaravans of Wiltshire. Mr Brian Fulwell was appointed receiver and manager and only one model would remain in production, based on the Commer. Company founder, Gareth Haylett, later joined Torcars as General Manager.

- Torcars issued a press release towards the end of the year confirming that the 500th Marina Sun-Tor had been built. The company's complete model range by the end of the year was as follows: Marina Sun-Tor, Marina Sun-Camper (no rising roof), Sherpa Sun-Tor, Commer Hi-Tor, Commer Hi-Tor Executive and Commer Major.

Many believe that Dormobile lost its direction with this model, the coach-built Toyota New World. Not one of the company's better designs from the 1970s.

This model, however, was far more successful, the Dormobile Deauville coach-build was available on Bedford CF and Sherpa bases.

■ The expected rise in sales to 22,000 units predicted the previous year proved to be somewhat optimistic. In fact, fewer than 8,000 units were sold in 1974. Motorcaravans on display at the London Motor Show near the end of this year included models by Auto-Sleepers, CI Autohomes, Danbury, Devon, European Caravans, Holdsworth, Newlander, Nimbus, Torcars and Suntrekker.

1976

■ The year was to begin with the loss of one of the oldest conversion companies, Cotswold. Quick to fill the void was K. J. Caravans of Hull with its coach-built Glendale. The first model was built upon the Leyland Sherpa, but when put into full production only the Bedford CF and Transit were used (with a handful built on the Toyota).

■ Released the previous year, the Sherpa was proving to be a popular base vehicle. Torcars announced a coach-built model, the Sherpa Royale, and Richard Holdsworth offered a panel van conversion with rising roof. A further model released at the end of the year was the Everest Sherpa by Endrust Auto-Truck Rustproofing Ltd. This was a very unusual model because the rear doors had been replaced with a fitted section (non opening); it also had a vinyl roof, tinted windows, sunroof and reclining seats.

■ The biggest surprise of the year was the end of the Commer Highwayman, the best-selling coach-built model in the UK throughout the 1960s. It was to re-emerge, however, completely restyled as the Sherpa Highwayman.

■ In July, VW announced a new van, the LT range. Devon was, unsurprisingly, the first to convert the new VW van. Bariban quickly followed and Suntrekker also released a demountable unit for the LT. One other demountable unit released this year was the Colin Reed Custom Camper. Very sporty in appearance, it was designed to fit the Marina pick-up; the price was £3,640, inclusive of VAT.

■ The year commenced with two conversion companies operating out of the small town of Torrington, Devon (Torcars and C&W Conversions). By the end of the year there was to be yet another, Euroconversions, which offered a Ford Escort camper that was not unlike their neighbour's Nimbus model.

■ One of the big surprises of the year was the release of a coach-built model (for the first time), by Auto-Sleepers Ltd. Based on the Bedford CF chassis, this model was given the designation CB22.

■ 1976 also heralded the demise of a very famous British transport name, Commer. Despite a change of name, the base vehicle would remain the same, as the Commer became the Dodge Spacevan.

■ Celebrities purchasing campers this year included Jimmy Saville, who traded in his Landliner for the new Transit CI Travelhome. 'Sooty and Sweep' creator, Harry Corbett, went to the Poole factory to pick up his CI Travelhome, while legendary rock drummer John Bonham of Led

The Glendale coach-built examples enjoyed huge sales success during the late 1970s and into the 1980s. They were available as both long and short wheelbase models and were built on a variety of chassis. The Bedford CF example pictured here dates from 1979.

Zeppelin purchased an Autobahn by Bariban, with a matching trailer.

- The industry released figures stating that coach-built models now accounted for one in five of all motorcaravans sold in the UK. CI Autohomes dominated the coach-built sector with 75 per cent of the market. CI announced that it was sending about 30 per cent of its total production abroad.
- Figures released this year indicated that the motorcaravan market was in decline, with 4,673 units being the total for 1975. In the space of just three years, the total units sold dropped from 15,000 to fewer than 5,000.

1977

- This was a year of consolidation within the industry after the falling sales of recent years. New models introduced included the Manzi-Gibbons VW, the Caribbean, which

were coach-built on a variety of chassis, and the Multicruiser demountable unit, again for a selection of base vehicles. Two new coach-built examples for this year were the Corvesgate (on several chassis) by Corvesgate Coachcraft and the Hi-Line by Humberside Interiors (on the Mercedes 306D).

- A novel introduction was the coach-built model based on the little Honda 350cc model; this was the Montrose at £3,600. But receiving greater accolades for the Honda base was the Barry Stimson designed Romahome; this was a GRP unit designed to fit onto the back of a Honda 350cc pick-up, price £2,750.
- Volkswagen campers were enjoying great sales success and two new models were launched this year. First, the Howard-Lange (London-based company) example fitted with the Argonaut rising roof, and second, a special model from Devon

Conversions. The Devon 21 was released to celebrate twenty-one years of Devon campers. It was based on the Eurovette Microbus model and given a paint finish in Oceanic Blue and white; interior upholstery and curtains were in matching colours. The Devon special was priced at £5,370. The same company was also enjoying great export success with its Eurovette model. These were being sold to France and Belgium, with the company stating that it had exported 900 campers in a two-year period.

- There was little in the way of new base vehicle releases this year, with manufacturers opting instead for modifications and improvements to existing models. Biggest of these changes was to the Chrysler Dodge Spacevan (Commer). This year it was given a new front plastic grille and lights; Chrysler was also forging ahead with a huge advertising

From the mid-1970s CI Autohomes of Poole dropped the use of its Parkestone rising roof on panel van conversions, opting instead for this spring-loaded roof which was then fitted to all the Trailblazer models. Displayed here on the Transit MK II, the Trailblazer was available on the Bedford CF, Commer and Sherpa.

Launched in the latter half of the 1970s, this Advantura coach-build was a massive success. It was offered as short and long wheelbase models and on several chassis. It is seen here on the Transit LWB chassis.

Torcars didn't have the monopoly on Morris Marina conversions. This is the Marina Suntrekker dismountable model. The company produced these detachable units for every chassis during the 1970s.

campaign for Dodge-based campers.

- A motorcaravan converter who had been absent from the listings for a couple of years made a return. Ivor Perry resurrected the Car-Camper models under the name of the Car-Camper Sales Company; this time the company was based in north Devon and was prepared to build on any base vehicle specified by the customer.
- Torcars, also in Devon, was now building a dozen Sun-Tor models a week; a press release stated that the works team could assemble a model in under eleven hours.
- Sales figures were released this year for the number of units sold in 1976; they were not good news for the industry, with only 3,811 motorcaravans being sold in total.

1978

- Whereas the previous year had been one of consolidation, this year would see the release of several new models and much more activity within the industry. One of the busiest on the new model scene was Richard Holdsworth releasing the coach-built Ranger on the Leyland Sherpa and the panel van conversion, the Hi-Flyer, with a GRP turtle-top style roof. Canterbury also released a turtle-top panel van, the Canterbury Sunhome.
- Dormobile brought out a coach-build this year based on the Sherpa, the Deauville. A far cry from the GRP models the Debonair and the Land Cruiser, the Deauville used traditional coachbuilding methods of aluminium panels over a hardwood frame.
- For some time, Devon Conversions had enjoyed the status of being the sole approved converter of VW vans, but this now changed with VW (GB) announcing that Bariban, Danbury and the Spacemaker Group would all be given official approval for new models. Devon released its new models the Moonraker and Sundowner this year, in addition to making use of the bigger VW LT base for the Devon Royalty.
- Newly appointed VW converter Bariban announced two new

models based on the Mercedes chassis, a rising-roof model at £6,537 and a high top at £9,153.
- CI Autohomes of Poole had a nine-model line-up by this time and announced an improved Travelhome MK III. At the motorcaravan of the year awards in Turin, CI Autohomes took the trophy for its Motorhome MK III, in the face of opposition from fifty other models. The company were also busy on the export market building the coach-built Gemini model for the French market. The Gemini was never made available in the UK and was sold in France through the distributor Sodis.
- A motorcaravan that was to prove very popular in the coming years, the Hymer, made an appearance this year. The Hymer 521 was based on the Bedford CF and was to be imported into the UK by Hymer Motorhomes of Sidcup.
- The very popular children's TV programme *Blue Peter* had connections with motorcaravans this year. Four CI Dodge Motorhomes were purchased from Madisons and modified for use as mobile classrooms for deaf children. Money to purchase the campers had been raised by *Blue Peter* viewers; the campers would have blue cabs and feature the *Blue Peter* shield on each cab door.
- Figures appearing in the motorcaravan press in relation to the previous year indicated that the Ford Transit accounted for 22 per cent of motorcaravans sold in the UK. The Bedford was listed at 18 per cent, with the little Fiat 900 in third spot and the VW in fourth. The Leyland Sherpa had crept up to fifth place, with the Toyota in sixth. It made sad reading for Chrysler, with the Dodge Spacevan slipping out of the top six for the first time. There was a marked improvement for the industry overall with sales for total units up on the previous year. The figure released for total sales in 1977 was 4,454.

1979

- As the 1970s reached its conclusion few of those original innovators

remained. In fact, the only two names to survive from the mid-1950s were Dormobile and Devon, although both had gone through many changes in that time. Bluebird Caravans, whose motorcaravan division became CI/Motorized and later CI Autohomes, was still one of the leading converters.
- On a par with CI Autohomes was the Spacemaker Group, which included Motorhomes International, Motorcaravan Conversions, Motorsleepers, Hilton Motorhomes and Viking Motorhomes. Model line-up included the Leyland Hustler, CF Mirage, Toyota Rio, Fiat Amigo, Leyland Buccaneer and VW Viking. They were all fitted with the Spacemaker rising roof, with the exception of the coach-built Hilton model.
- Danbury had been around for many years, firstly converting the VW, then the Toyota and finally winning back VW approval once more for VW conversions. This year the company would also begin to use the Ford Transit, but the man behind Danbury's success, George Dawson, sadly passed away.
- Other notable items of news from this year included the release of the Pampas Nevada on the VW LT, and the introduction of the MK II Romahome, which by now was available on the Suzuki as well as on the Honda. CI Autohomes released a MK II version of its Sherpa Highwayman, Auto-Sleepers redesigned its rising roof and incorporated a GRP roof rack, and a name from the past, J.H. Jennings, built a one-off luxury Roadranger for a client, based on the big Mercedes. By far the biggest news item of the year came from Volkswagen, which announced the new T25 range.
- The industry released the sales figure for 1978 this year, a steady increase once more, this time up to 4,725. The figure for 1979 would be an increase yet again, up to 4,917 units. This figure would continue to fluctuate throughout the 1980s and 1990s, though never achieving the heady success of the early 1970s (pre-VAT).

classic motorcaravanning today

No classic campers receive more publicity than the famous VW models. Spares are plentiful and the enthusiasm for them remains as strong today as it has always been.

WHAT DEFINES A CLASSIC?

There is quite a clear point at which classic motorcaravans and campers begin, and that is with the early 1950s examples. It is at the opposite end of the scale that there is much heated debate – is there a cut-off date for classic campers? It isn't a debate that is restricted to classic campers; the whole classic vehicle world (in the UK at least) is constantly calling for a more definitive answer, and quite rightly so. Both the veteran and vintage enthusiasts were given clarity on this issue many years ago; a veteran vehicle is one that was built up to (and including) December 1918, while vintage covers the period between January 1919 and December 1930. Classic vehicles therefore fall into the period of 1930 to an undetermined moment in time. At the time of writing, vehicles constructed up to the end of December 1972 are classified as 'historic' for the purposes of the road fund taxation scheme (in the UK). Some argue that this is a correct date for classic designation, but others argue, with some justification, that identical vehicles built either side of this date

Classic camper enthusiasts belong to a variety of specialist owners clubs in the UK. They often spend the summer months meeting up at rallies around the country.

are both classic. Some of the classic vehicle fraternity are more understanding, arguing that chrome fittings such as bumpers, mirrors, lights and so forth are also typical of classic identification. If this were the case, then many chrome exterior fittings were being phased out as the 1970s came to a close, probably

for the sake of economizing by the manufacturers.

Visit a classic vehicle show or steam rally during the summer months and chances are that you will see vehicles on display that were constructed well into the late 1980s. It is an issue on which the classic vehicle movement is

The major problem facing owners of classic examples today is the search for spares and good used parts. Autojumbles are a good source, held throughout the year both outside and indoors.

deeply divided, although there is a reasonable amount of acceptance and tolerance in all quarters. I will certainly not attempt to resolve the issue within this book; it is simply my duty as an author to point out the facts, as I understand them.

CLASSIC CAMPERS – DINOSAURS OR PRACTICAL LEISURE VEHICLES?

Can a motorcaravan built twenty, thirty or forty years ago still be a practical proposition for modern camping forays? In these days of high-technological advances it is quite easy to forget why campers and motorhomes were first conceived. They were a means of enjoying the great outdoors, living close to nature, exploring different locations both in the UK and abroad. The BMC J2s, Ford Thames, Bedford CAs and the like *were* the transport of the day back then, and these vehicles incorporated all that was new into their designs. It is little wonder then that people had no worries at the time about jumping into a BMC Paralanian or Bluebird Highwayman, then taking off around the UK or even abroad to

explore the boundaries of foreign lands. Those vehicles were capable of such feats then and they still are today.

The difference is that we now, of course, have modern campers to compare them to. Their modern counterparts are certainly quicker and probably more economical; as for comfort, the Paralanian, Jennings Roadranger and similar models remain as comfortable today as they were in their heyday. It is true that modern campers have much more in the way of creature comforts, such as luxury washrooms, reversing cameras, solar-assisted aids, cruise control and so forth. But many of these features can easily be fitted in retrospect to older vehicles. In fact, the owners of many coach-built models are now upgrading their engines from the fuel-guzzling petrol units to very economical diesel units from more modern vans. This is, in turn, extending both the life of the older camper vans and the enjoyment one can get from using them. In short, classic motorcaravans are enjoying something of a renaissance period today.

If there is one drawback to ownership of a classic example (other than the

Volkswagen), it is the situation in relation to spare parts, both mechanical items and bodywork. The vast majority of items can no longer simply be ordered from the local main dealer and picked up the next day. It really is now a case of hunting around such places as autojumbles, shows, local motor factors and vehicle breakers; last but not least, there is always the Internet.

I did just mention one exception to the rule in relation to spares, the evergreen Volkswagen in its various forms. This vehicle really is in a class of its own, not only in the parts area, but in general global appeal. It is now a cult vehicle, adored by millions the world over, and that dedicated following shows no signs of slowing down with each subsequent new generation. In the 1950s it was new and very different, in the 1960s it had become synonymous with the flower-power era, but by the 1970s it had strong associations with the surf brigade. The early split-windscreen models in particular are one of the most sought-after vehicles in the world today; even a model requiring major restoration can change hands for several thousand pounds sterling. That very model went out of

ABOVE: The owner of this Paralanian couldn't resist the temptation to copy the modern motorcaravanners who are often seen towing small cars behind their large RV models. Horses for courses, this Parry tows another Austin, the A30 variant.

production more than forty years ago, yet it is still used by pop and rock bands to promote their videos and by advertising executives for TV commercials. Its appeal is simply staggering and unquantifiable. The popularity of this early VW has had a knock-on effect within classic camper circles of late. Because of the incredible prices that they are realizing, prospective owners have begun to look at other campers of the period. As a consequence, the prices of Commer, Bedford and early Transit campers have risen dramatically.

Of course, it would be foolhardy even to suggest that any of the UK-derived campers would, or could, ever rival the early VW on the global used vehicle market. But certainly in the UK other examples are appreciating annually. Of these, the Bedford CF, Commer and Ford Transit MK I and MK II are the campers with the most appeal to anyone seeking a good usable classic motorcaravan. Spare parts for each of

Interest in classic campers has increased dramatically in recent years; they are now an established part of the classic scene in the UK. This was a display of classics at an NEC classic car show.

them are still fairly easy to track down, although replacement body panels are in very short supply. Old stock panels do occasionally surface, but more often than not it is a case of getting a repair section made up by a fabricator.

In terms of being driver-friendly, then possibly the Bedford CF and Transit offer the best 'car-like' handling and driver comfort. The Commer is best described as 'quirky', though it has an endearing quality about it and is often regarded as a 'love it or loathe it' type of vehicle.

Certainly in panel van form with a rising roof, it is probably the closest externally to the early VW models. Internally it offers far more usable space due to its twin opening rear doors and front (cab) mounted engine. Both the Bedford CF and Transit offer the owner wonderful upgrading opportunities. The CF was in production until 1987 as the CF2, and often parts from later vehicles can be fitted to earlier examples. The same applies to the Transit, and probably more so, such was the array of

In order to get full enjoyment out of the older models, it is sometimes necessary to update them a little. This delightful Bedford CF Auto-Sleeper was rescued from the scrap yard, then fully restored and given a modern paint finish. Clarice the camper is a regular sight now on the classic scene.

different engine options offered by Ford throughout production. The most obvious change made by many owners of the MK I-based Transit campers is to replace the petrol engine with a diesel unit from a much later Transit. This gives the owner far greater mpg, but does require the fitting of the bull-nose Transit front panels in order to accommodate the often bigger diesel engine.

If a couple or single person is looking for a show/picnic camper, then there are countless models to choose from in the micro-camper category. The Marina Sun-Tor models are now a little thin on the ground, but plenty of the earlier BMC A55/60 Sun-Tors have survived. Parts availability is also quite good for the Escort-derived campers, so the likes of the Dormobile Elba, Canterbury Siesta, Freedom camper and Nimbus are a good proposition.

If space and luxury are high on the agenda, then the BMC/Commer Paralanian, Jennings Roadranger and Commer Tourstar would easily meet the demands of most people. Purely for investment purposes, the early VW is head and shoulders above everything else. Next on the list of sound

There is no better sight during the summer months than a line of colourful classic motorcaravans, as this picture clearly illustrates.

These winning models were pictured at the annual national meeting of the Classic Camper Club, where each year members vote for their favourite models in various categories. Pictured here from right to left are: Dormobile Debonair, Commer Jennings Roadranger, Commer Tourstar, Commer-Commer and Bedford CF Auto-Sleeper CB22.

investments must be the VW T2 with a conversion by Dormobile. Other than VW campers the best buys are always the low-mileage, one- or two-owner examples that have been dry-stored throughout ownership. There is one camper that is highly prized by both classic camper enthusiasts and Mini fanatics, the Mini Wildgoose. In fact, a very well-restored model could even give some early VW campers a run for their money in the asking-price stakes!

There are numerous owners clubs in existence catering for classic campers. Some are quite general in catering for any vehicle from the period, while others are more specialized and cater for a particular converter or make of base vehicle. There is little point in publishing contact details here for any such organizations, as contact details may frequently change. Up-to-date details can be found in most monthly classic vehicle magazines and motorcaravan publications. Failing that, the use of a good search engine on the Internet will probably yield some useful results.

appendix

AN A TO Z OF THE MAIN MOTORCARAVAN CONVERTERS, 1956–79

Airborne
Associated Caravans
Autochalet
Auto-Homes
Auto-Kabins
Autoroam

Bariban
Bedmobile
Bluebird (later CI/Motorized, then CI Autohomes)

Calthorpe
Caraversions
Caraville
Carawagon
Car-Campers
Caribbean Motorhomes
Catford Motor Caravan Centre
Central Garage
Coachwork Conversions
Commer
Cooper & Griffin
Corvesgate Coachcraft
C&W Conversions

Danbury
Dandy Caravans
Drive Hire Mobile Holiday Units (Caraboot)

Euroconversions
European Caravans (Motorized)
European Cars

Fairthorpe

Haylett Motor Caravans
Holdsworth (Richard)
Hosking
Howard-Lange

Jennings, J. H.

Kenex
Kingscote & Stephens (Cotswold)
K. J. Caravans

Landcruisers
Locomotors

Madisons
Martin Walter
Moortown Motors
Motor Caravan Bodies
M.T.S.
Murray Pickaback

National Motorhome Centre
Newlander
Nomad

Oxley Coachcraft

Perthshire Caravan Company
Peter Pitt (Later Canterbury-Pitt, them Canterbury)

Ryan

Service
Spacemaker Group

Torcars
Turner (D.) Garages

Walker B. & Son
Wessex
Whitehall
Wildgoose Worthing
Wilsons
Wordsworth Investments

York Motor Caravan Company

This list represents the vast majority of conversion companies from the classic period. In addition, there would have been many small coachbuilding operations offering to build one-off models, or very limited production runs.

further reading

Wilkinson, T. *Motor Caravanning*
(David & Charles, 1968)
This book contains some interesting model profiles, line drawings and excellent photographs. Again written as a guide for the period, it now represents a very good reference guide for classic followers.

Lyons, S. *Motorcaravanning at Home and Abroad*
(Yeoman Publications Ltd, 1973)
This book is really more of a 'How to' publication. It contains few photographs, but instead relies completely on cartoon drawings by 'Nardi' of humorous camping moments.

Myhill, H. *Motor Caravanning*
(Ward Lock Ltd, 1976)
Written by long-time motorcaravanner and writer Henry Myhill, who incidentally lived in a Bluebird Highwayman for several years. Although written as a guide for motorcaravanners of the period, it is now of interest to classic camper enthusiasts simply because of the models mentioned in the text and the photographs that it contains.

Park, C. *The Complete Book of Motorcaravanning*
(Haynes, 1979)
An excellent large format book, which because of its publication date is especially interesting to classic camper enthusiasts. It is once again a guide to motorcaravanning, but is packed with photographs of classic models.

Hunt, J. *The Practical Motorcaravanner*
(David & Charles, 1983)
Written by one of the most respected motorcaravan journalists in the UK, John Hunt. John introduced the first monthly magazine for motorcaravanners to go on sale to the public in 1966. Many models were altered by the conversion company after John had road-tested the prototype and pointed out the shortcomings! This book was a guide to motorcaravanning, but makes reference to many of the models and base vehicles of the classic period.

Wilson, N. *Gypsies and Gentlemen*
(Columbus Books, 1986)
Not of great interest to classic enthusiasts, but a fascinating book for anyone interested in the development of caravanning, camping and motorcaravanning. A very good historical book tracing the camping culture from early horse-drawn wagons through to Field Marshal Montgomery's motorhomes that he used during World War II.

Hanson, J. *The Story of the Motor Caravan*
(Malvern House Publications, 1997)
The smallest of all the books mentioned here, this was produced in A5 format in the style of a booklet. Northern-based transport historian John Hanson is a dedicated enthusiast of vintage, veteran and classic motorcaravans and owns several himself. Although small in size, this book contains many excellent photographs, a large proportion of which were published for the first time in this book.

Eccles, D. *VW Camper – The Inside Story*
(The Crowood Press, 2005)
Highly regarded as one of the best books of its type by both VW camper fanatics and motoring historians. For my part, I believe it to be the very best book available, detailing nearly every model of VW camper between 1951 and 2005. No Volkswagen camper owner, enthusiast or fan can afford not to have this on his or her bookshelf.

Trant, K. *'Home Away from Home'*
(Black Dog Publishing, 2006)
Despite being the largest book of all those mentioned here, it is a curious publication as it doesn't easily fall into a specific category. It is certainly not a guidebook, but more of a reference book taking a look at owners and their campers, both in the UK and the USA. Although aimed heavily at the American market, it does contain many UK-based owners describing their campers and why they enjoy using them.

owners' clubs catering for classic models

Amigo and Friends Association (Fiat Amigo, Caravelle, Fargo, Fiesta and Pandora)
Kevin Graves
47 Horseshoe Lane
Kirton
Boston
Lincs PE20 1LJ
www.fiatamigo.co.uk

Auto-Sleeper Owners' Club (all Auto-Sleeper models)
Norma Caley
17 Rydal Avenue
Freckleton
Preston PR4 1DJ
www.asoc.fsnet.co.uk

Bedford Owners' Club International (Bedford models)
Mike Knowles
27 Northville Drive
Westcliff-on-Sea
Essex SS0 0QA

Camping and Caravanning Club (all campers and caravans)
Greenfields House
Westwood Way
Coventry CV4 8JH
www.campingandcaravanningclub.co.uk

Camping & Caravan Club, motorcaravan section (all motorcaravans)
Mrs Kathy Giles
8 Herons Close
Chilham
Canterbury
Kent CT4 8DN
www.campingandcaravanclub.co.uk

Caravan Club (all motorcaravans)
East Grinstead House
East Grinstead
West Sussex RH19 1UA
www.caravanclub.co.uk

Classic Camper Club (all motorcaravans built prior to 1987)
Sue Mickleborough
PO Box 155
Dartford
Kent DA2 7WU
www.classiccamperclub.co.uk

Dormobile Owners' Club (genuine Dormobile motorcaravans)
Mr A Horne
23 Fairmile
Aylesbury HP21 7JS
www.dormobile.org.uk

Holdsworth Owners' Club (all Holdsworth models)
Christine Chamberlain
14 Barracks Lane
Shirehampton
Bristol BS11 9NG

Landliner Club (Ford Transit Landliner models by CI/M)
Brian Stubbs
13 Oakwood Drive
Lordswood
Southampton SO1 8EJ

Motor Caravanners' Club (all motorcaravans)
Colin Reay
22 Evelyn Close
Twickenham
Middlesex TW2 7BN
www.motorcaravanners.org.uk

Period Motorcaravan Guild (all models produced before 1973)
John Hanson
116 Copgrove Road
Leeds LS8 2RS
www.brmmbrmm.com/periodmcg

Splitscreen Van Club (all 'splitty' VW campers)
Mike and Sue Mundy
Welbeck House
Manor Road
Burgess Hill
Sussex RH16 0NW
www.ssvc.org.uk

Sprite Motorhome Club (Sprite Motorhomes produced by CI/M)
Mrs Jo Arbeiters
30 White Cross
Peterborough PE3 7LP

Torcars Sun-Tor Register (all motorcaravans built by Torcars of Torrington)
Jim Matthews
35 Walkerith Road
Morton
Gainsborough DN21 3DA
www.brmmbrmm.com/torcars

Victor 101 Club (all Bedford CA- and CF-based campers)
Gerry and Joan Caldwell
43 Princess Street
Widnes
Cheshire WA8 6NT
www.motorbase.com/contact/by-id/1048

Volkswagen Type 2 Owners Club (all Type 2 campers)
Phil Shaw
57 Humphrey Avenue
Charford
Bromsgrove B60 3JD
www.vwt2oc.org

VW LT Motorhome Club (all campers based on the VW LT base)
Graham Sedgwick
No. 2 Lodge
Northside Caravan Park
North Road
Carnforth LA6 1AA

Please note that the contact details listed for the various clubs are likely to change periodically. I would suggest that you consult one of the motorcaravan publications available from most newsagents. Nearly all the clubs listed arrange meetings throughout the year, and produce a club journal/newsletter for their members. In addition to these clubs, there are a large number of Internet-based forums for older campers.

Complimenting the specialist motorcaravan clubs listed, there are a very small number of motorcaravans within the two leading trailer caravan clubs for older models. These are:

The Historic Caravan Club (caters for pre-1961 models)
Ron Squires
'Arwel'
Victoria Road
Llanwrtd Wells
Powys LD5 4SU
www.hcclub.co.uk

Period and Classic Caravan Club (trailer caravans over 25 years of age)
Jill Rumbelow
128 Fulbourn Old Drift
Cherry Hinton
Cambridgeshire CB1 9LR
www.period-classic-caravan-club.co.uk

index